NINE
A SALUTE TO MR. HOCKEY

Copyright© 2007 Olympia Entertainment Inc.

All Rights Reserved. No part of this book may be reproduced, stored in a retrieval system or transmitted, in any form by any means, electronically, mechanically, photocopying or otherwise, without prior written permission from the publisher, Olympia Entertainment, 2211 Woodward Avenue, Detroit, Michigan 48201.

Executive Editor: Mike Bayoff   **Managing Editor:** Bill Roose
Authors: Bob Duff, Bill Roose   **Copy Editor:** Michael Passman, Bill Roose
Creative Design: Craig C. Wheeler, CFW Creative Sports, Inc.
Produced by: CFW Creative Sports, Inc.

All photos were provided by the Howe family, except where noted. Every reasonable attempt was made to give proper credit. If there are any errors, please notify the publisher and corrections will be made in subsequent editions.

Acknowledgements: Mark Dehem, Gibraltar Trade Center; Felix Gatt, Creative Impressions; Wendy McCreary and Debbie Sittler, NHL Alumni Association; Lindsey Ungar

Special thanks: Jeff Altstadter, New Jersey Devils; Sharon Arend, Ilitch Holdings; Lauren Baxter, Carolina Hurricanes; Craig Campbell, Hockey Hall of Fame; Kevin Crawley, Phoenix Coyotes; Jim DeMaria, Chicago Blackhawks; Craig Downey, Toronto Maple Leafs; Allen Einstein, Detroit Pistons; Scott Henninger, Houston Aeros; Rejean Houle, Montreal Canadiens; Imperial Oil-Turofsky, Hockey Hall of Fame; Jim Johnson, Companions in Courage Foundation; Jean Martineau, Colorado Avalanche; Tom McMillan, Pittsburgh Penguins; Paul Michinard, Getty Images; Dave Reginek; Dale Saip, Vancouver Giants; Dave Sandford, Hockey Hall of Fame; Aaron Sickman, Minnesota Wild; Bob Sweeney, Boston Bruins; Diana Taylor, Philadelphia Flyers; Bill Wickett, Tampa Bay Lightning; Corey Witt, New York Islanders.

Very special thanks: Mark Howe, Marty Howe, Murray Howe, Travis Howe

Library of Congress Control Number: 2007934836
ISBN: 0-9664120-9-5
ISBN 13: 9780966412093

Printed in the United States

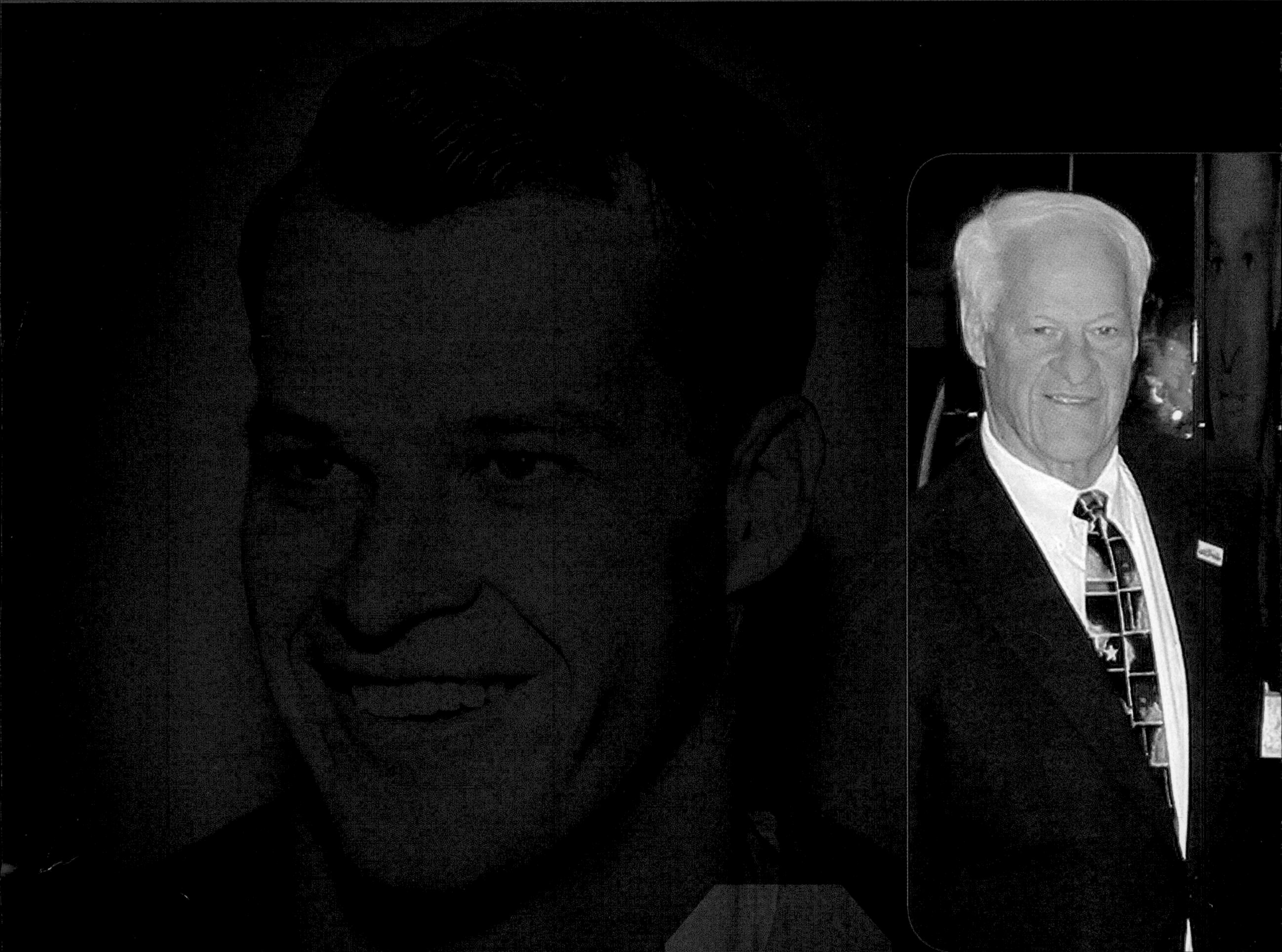

Dear Hockey Fans Everywhere,

Like all hockey fans, we have admired Gordie Howe (Mr. Hockey) and have applauded his career for years. He is a legend in Detroit and throughout the game of hockey.

Gordie joined the Red Wings in 1946 when he was only 18 years of age and remained with the team for 25 seasons. He was named to 21 All-Star teams (an NHL record) and led Detroit to four Stanley Cup championships. His stats and numerous awards are legendary and will remain documented in the record books forever.

We have personally known Gordie for most of our adult lives and have been able to experience, first hand, many of his milestones in a hockey career that spanned six decades. It amazes us that he was able to play the physically intense game of hockey until the age of 52.

When we created the Gordie Howe entrance at Joe Louis Arena in 2006 and commissioned his bronze statue, we created an immortal tribute to one of the greatest hockey players of all time. But we were also honoring a dear friend, who has touched our lives personally. He has a big heart, and whenever we asked something of Gordie, he always willingly responded and never asked for anything in return. He is a great ambassador for the game of hockey and a wonderful role model to aspiring young hockey players. He and his wife, Colleen (Mrs. Hockey), have dedicated their lives to the game of hockey and to worthwhile causes benefiting young people.

Nine: A Salute to Mr. Hockey, Gordie Howe captures some of the most memorable moments of his outstanding hockey career. For the mature readers, we hope you will relive some of your personal Gordie Howe memories. For the younger readers, we know you will be inspired, as you better understand the talent of this great hockey player. Gordie Howe has definitely earned the right to

There have been many stories written about Gordie Howe and a lot of comparing his hockey talents to other players in different eras. For me, he was the best I ever played against, the best I ever played with, and the best friend a guy could have.

We go back to 1946 when we both broke into the NHL — Gord with the Red Wings and me with the Chicago Black Hawks. I outscored him in our rookie season and then he 'took off'. I actually played more games with him in five seasons with the Red Wings than I played against in 15 seasons.

Not only was Gord a superstar on the ice, he was a great ambassador for the hockey league, and still is, always willing to sign autographs for hours. He's friendly to all, especially the children. He would correct them if they were rude; I've often heard him ask a youngster if he or she knew how to say 'please' and 'thank you'. He has been involved in countless charities, giving of his time and energy.

As a friend, we have much in common. We share the love of our families. Our wives — Colleen and Edna — are best friends. Our memories over the past 50 years could fill a book -- vacations, fishing trips to Florida, Hawaii, Panama, Ecuador, Canada, northern Michigan, weddings, birthdays, anniversaries, and more. There have also been sad times when we have been there for each other.

Gord has always been devoted and protective of his family, but in recent years he has showed courage and patience while caring for his beloved wife Colleen, who suffers from Pick's disease, a rare and horrible form of dementia. Although she doesn't recognize us anymore, we still visit every Sunday after church. Gord and I often recall the past and need each other if our memories slip.

I know first hand, how generous he is. Recently, I had a couple of rough years. I had a double-bypass in September 2005 and an abdominal aortic aneurysm in January 2006. My book, "The Grateful Gadsby" was out that season and I was scheduled to do a book signing at Joe Louis Arena. Gord and our friend Felix Gatt of Creative Impressions had a big sign made-up, and not only did they sell lots of books that Gord personalized, they had fans write get-well messages to me on the sign. The next day, Gord arrived at the hospital, had all of the nurses and doctors sign it, and put the sign on display for all to see.

It's amazing. He's recognized easily and still creates quite a stir when he walks in anywhere.

He deserves every honor that he's ever received. I'm happy he and Colleen came into our lives.

God bless you my friend!

Love,

Edna and Bill Gadsby

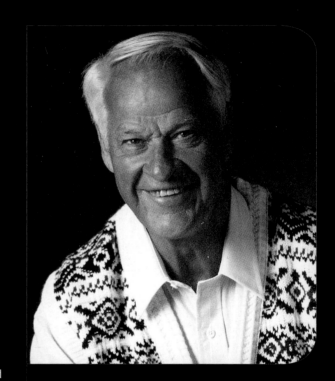

I dedicate this book to my lovely bride Colleen. While I received the applause, you stood behind me and cheered the loudest. While I focused on improving my game, you made sure the bills were getting paid. While I was on the overnight trains and planes from city to city, you were tucking in the kids and teaching them to pray for their daddy. You have been my biggest fan. My agent. My dietician. My counselor. And even now as you battle for your life, you are my inspiration, my strength, and the love of my life.

I love you very much,

NINE

It's a story that began when I was a young punk, rookie kid. We played the Red Wings in our third or so game of the season. I went over to check Gordie Howe, and I think I went to lift his stick, and caught him on his cheekbone. It looked like there was just a little scratch or something, but there was a whistle on the play. He looks down and sees a little blood on the ice. He looked at me, and I'm kind of smiling I guess, and he points his finger at me. When he did that, I said, 'Ah, get out of here you old bastard, you should of retired years ago. You're too old for this game anyway.'

"We're in the dressing room between periods, and Ted Lindsay is sitting next to me and says, 'Stanley, you shouldn't have talked to Gordie the way you did.' I said, 'Well, he is old. He shouldn't be out here.' And he said, 'What you just said, he'll never forget. Watch yourself.'

"We get to a game in Detroit, about five, six or seven games after the incident, and I had kind of forgotten about it. Gordie came skating back after we had shot the puck in the end zone, and I'm going in to fore-check. I cut across the middle and the next thing I know, I've got an awfully sore jaw. I'm rolling around and don't know where the hell I am. I see a bunch of guys sitting on the bench, so I literally started crawling over there. I get on the bench and in about two-seconds I feel somebody lifting me up under the armpits. The next thing I know they're throwing me over the boards onto the ice. I ended up on the Red Wings' bench. That's how goofy I was.

STAN MIKITA | Center, 1958-80
1983 HOF Inductee

GORDIE HOWE
"MR. HOCKEY"

BORN: MARCH 31, 1928 – FLORAL, SASKATCHEWAN, CANADA

USHL OMAHA KNIGHTS – 1945/46
NHL DETROIT RED WINGS – 1946/47 – 1970/71
WHA HOUSTON AEROS – 1973/74 – 1976/77
WHA NEW ENGLAND WHALERS – 1977/78 – 1978/79
NHL HARTFORD WHALERS – 1979/80
IHL DETROIT VIPERS – 1997/98 ONE GAME, ONE SHIFT

GORDIE HOWE IS REGARDED AS ONE OF THE GREATEST HOCKEY PLAYERS OF ALL TIME, KNOWN FOR HIS SCORING PROWESS, PHYSICAL STRENGTH AND LONGEVITY. HE JOINED THE RED WINGS IN 1946 AT THE AGE OF 18 AND REMAINED WITH THE TEAM FOR 25 SEASONS. HE LED DETROIT TO FOUR STANLEY CUP CHAMPIONSHIPS AND TO FIRST PLACE IN REGULAR SEASON PLAY FOR SEVEN CONSECUTIVE YEARS FROM 1948/49 TO 1955/56. HE WAS NAMED TO 21 ALL-STAR TEAMS – AN NHL RECORD. HOWE SERVED AS CAPTAIN FROM 1958/59 – 1961/62. HIS NUMBER 9 WAS RETIRED ON MARCH 21, 1972, AND HE WAS INDUCTED INTO THE HOCKEY HALL OF FAME THE SAME YEAR.

HOWE AND HIS WIFE COLLEEN (MRS. HOCKEY) HAVE DEDICATED THEIR LIVES TO HOCKEY BOTH ON AND OFF THE ICE AND HAVE SUPPORTED MANY WORTHWHILE CAUSES BENEFITING YOUNG PEOPLE. THEY HAVE BEEN GREAT AMBASSADORS FOR THE SPORT OF HOCKEY.

SCULPTOR: OMNI R. AMRANY, 2007

NINE

Howe it *Began*

A hockey legend blooms
in a small Canadian
prairie town

t didn't start with a flash, or a burst of brilliance, but rather a staccato clomp, clomp, clomp.

That was the sound Gordie Howe's feet made when he came into the kitchen of the family home in Saskatoon.

So enamored with the game of hockey was young

inhale a sandwich before taking stick in hand and returning to the ice.

From such dedication, a hockey hero was born.

At first, Howe skated on one foot, forced to share the pair of skates his family purchased at the height of the Great Depression from another local family in

> He was quite the teaser. When he would come home for the summers, before he married Colleen, we would make our sandwiches for work the night before. Then when we got there, the bread was there, but the ham and cheese was gone. He would steal the good stuff and all we had was bread. We fell for that trick a couple of times.

JOAN CLARK Gordie's Sister

Born in Floral, a tiny wheat-farming town on the outskirts of Saskatoon, the family relocated to a home in nearby Saskatoon that Howe's dad, Ab, purchased for $650 when Gordie was all of nine days old.

His talents quickly emerged in the Saskatoon minor hockey system. Longtime friend and National Hockey League rival Johnny Bower grew up playing goal in nearby Prince Albert and remembered what it was like to face Howe back then.

"We just couldn't beat Gordie Howe and his teams," Bower said. "One time, we lost 8-2 and

Howe, he got more than a hat-trick on me. I think he ended up with five goals."

In 1943, Howe, 15, attended his first NHL training camp, in Winnipeg with the Rangers. "I was there four days," Howe recalled.

Howe was a youngster during the 1930s, when money was scarce. Growing up, catalogues replaced shin pads as hockey equipment.

``My first day in camp with the Rangers, I watched the guy beside me get dressed, to see where everything went," Howe said.

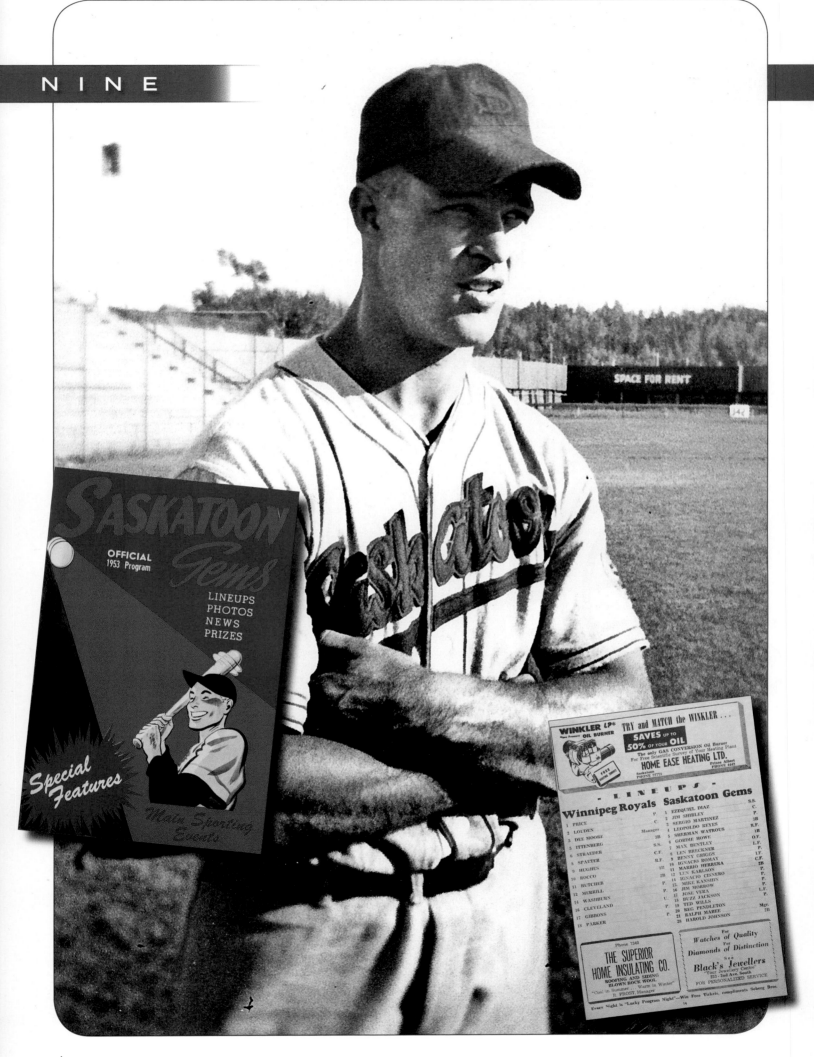

SASKATOON Gems

OFFICIAL
1953 Program

LINEUPS
PHOTOS
NEWS
PRIZES

Special Features

Main Sporting Events

SPACE FOR RENT

- LINEUPS -

Winnipeg Royals		Saskatoon Gems	
		1 EZEQUIEL DIAZ	S.S.
		2 JIM SHIRLEY	C.
1 PRICE	P.	3 SERGIO MARTINEZ	2B.
2 LOUDEN	C.	4 LEOPOLDO REYES	R.F.
3 DEE MOORE	Manager	5 SHERMAN WATROUS	1B.
5 ITTENBERG	3B	6 GORDIE HOWE	O.F.
6 STRAEDER	S.S.	7 MAX BENTLEY	L.F.
8 SPAETER	C.F.	8 LEN BRECKNER	P.
9 HUGHES	R.F.	9 BENNY GRIGGS	I.F.
10 ROCCO	1B.	10 IGNACIO ROMAY	C.F.
11 BUTCHER	2B.	11 MARIO HERRERA	2B.
12 MERRILL	P.	12 LUS KARLSON	P.
14 WASHBURN	P.	14 IGNACIO CISNERO	P.
16 CLEVELAND	P.	15 MIKE KANSHIN	P.
17 GIBBONS	P.	16 JIM MORROW	L.F.
21 PARKER	P.	17 JOSE VERA	P.
		18 BUZZ JACKSON	U.
		19 REG PENDLETON	Mgr.
		20 RALPH MABEE	2B
		28 HAROLD JOHNSON	

"When I was with New York, I knew Detroit was trying to make a deal for me, a trade. I took Gordie in the corner one night when we were playing, and he said, 'Hey big guy, lighten up a little bit, you're coming here tomorrow.' And I looked at him and said, 'Oh, yeah, yeah, yeah.' But it's true. I was walking off the ice after the game, and our general manager let me in the door and said, 'I just made a trade for you to Detroit.' Gordie knew about it before I did.

"He was a good teammate and a great friend. He did everything right on the ice; he didn't have too many bad nights. He back-checked, he killed penalties, he scored goals, he set-up goals. The best I ever played against."

BILL GADSBY
Defenseman, 1946-66
1970 HOF Inductee

"Art Ross, who coached and was the manager of the Boston Bruins, was telling me a story one time when Jack Adams was coaching the Detroit club. For some reason or other, they were talking about trades, and Mr. Ross told me that he said to Jack, 'That big, skinny looking guy' — Gordie wasn't really built to any great extent when he first started — but Ross said, 'That skinny guy, he's not doing anything right now. I'm interested in him, who do you want for him?' And Jack Adams said, 'No, I'm gonna stick with him for a while longer.'

"Gordie was very strong and he just had a tremendous shot. He was very accurate around the net. He was a strong skater, physically strong. He was one of those players, you had to watch him, there's no doubt about that. You couldn't leave him alone. I think a lot of people got in trouble doing that instead of minding your own business and letting him mind his own business.

MILT SCHMIDT | Center, 1936-55
1961 HOF Inductee

Another hockey legend, Lester Patrick, who was the Howe of his era, coming out of retirement to play goal during the 1928 Stanley Cup final, ran the Rangers when the teenaged Howe showed up amidst dozens of other prospects. "He spoke to me four times," Howe said. "At the start of camp, he asked, 'What's your name, son?' and then they wrote it on a piece of paper and pinned it to the back of my sweater.

"The first day, I hit (Rangers veteran) Grant Warwick with a pretty good bodycheck, and Mr. Patrick called me over and asked, 'What's your name, son?' Two other times, when I did something on the ice, he called me over and asked 'What's your name, son?' Finally, I said, 'It's on the back of my shirt, sir.' "

Unsigned and homesick, Howe returned to Saskatoon. The following fall, was invited to the Wings' training camp in Windsor, Ontario. He was assigned to Detroit's Ontario Hockey Association junior club in Galt, but wasn't allowed to play because the Saskatchewan association wouldn't permit him a transfer. He practiced all season with the team and participated in exhibition contests, learning the game from Al Murray, once an NHL defenseman with the New York Americans.

"He came to me and said, 'I've got some news for you, and you're not going to like it,' " Howe

remembered. "That's when he told me my transfer didn't come through. But he told me if I stayed the year in Galt, he'd make me into a hockey player, and he did."

Howe turned pro in 1945, playing for coach Tommy Ivan with Omaha of the U.S. League, scoring 22 goals and earning a spot on the second all-star team. The next spring, Ivan was promoted to Indianapolis of the American Hockey League.

Before training camp that fall, Detroit coach-GM Jack Adams told Ivan that Howe would be joining him at Indianapolis.

"No," Ivan said. "He'll be playing for you."

He was right.

"
I never had a tussle with him in the corners or anything, but man, he was hard to check. You just hoped that he made the mistake and not you. You knew if you got close to him you were in trouble. You tried to keep him to the outside, but you never tried to hit him and bowl him over because he would make you look silly. You tried to get as close as you could to him, like a magnet and attach yourself, opposed to trying to knock him over. I never saw anybody knock him over or take a run at him because it was well-known that his right arm was always up. I think he would adapt to whatever style today, but we will never see another player like Gordie, who can control the game. "

PIERRE PILOTE   Defenseman, 1955-69
1975 HOF Inductee

"His strength and his ability and the desire to perform the best that he could in every game made Gordie very special. I always had a lot of respect for Gordie. He was not only an asset for the Wings, but an asset for the league and for this great game of hockey.

"People kind of forget that in his second year, he had some kind of a skull fracture in a game against Toronto. After that, he kept everybody way from him. So, don't forget, it's very difficult when you have somebody on you all of the time. But, because of his great talent, his desire to win, and his physical strength it made him certainly one of the great hockey players."

JEAN BELIVEAU
Center, 1950-71
1972 HOF Inductee

NINE

A Near-Fatal Ending

Howe's Red Wings days are
nearly over when they've
barely started

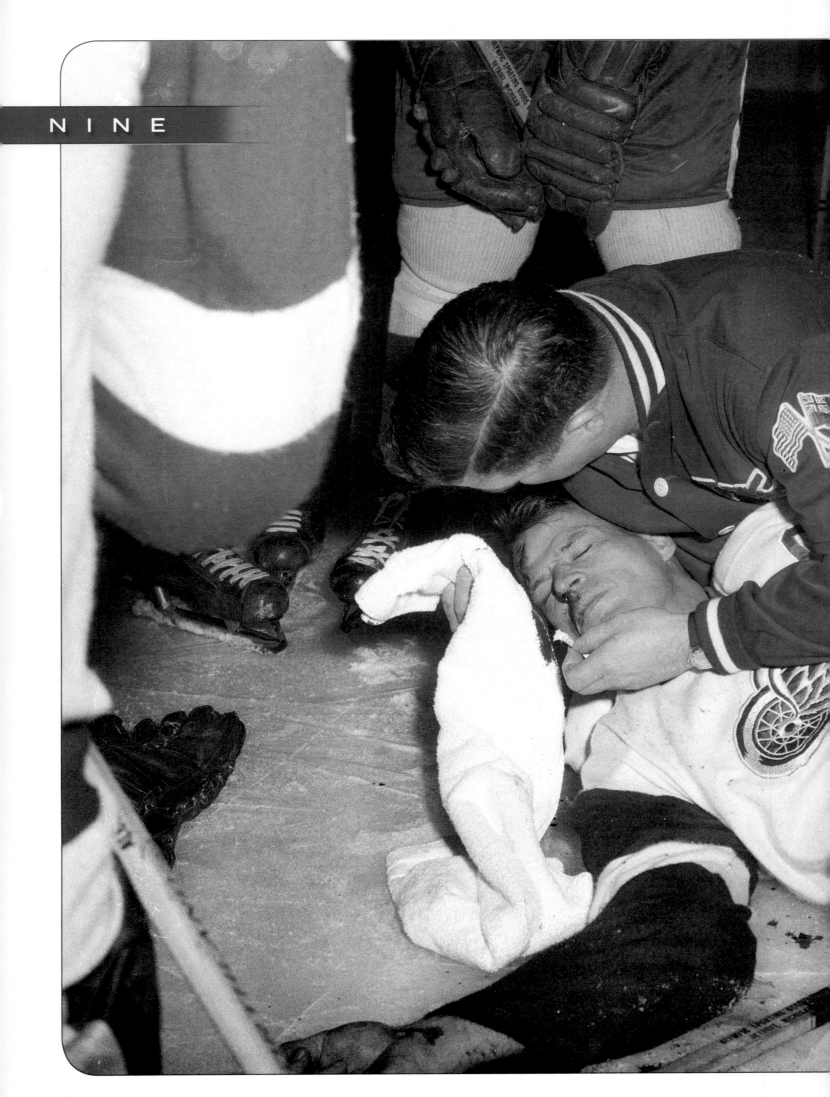

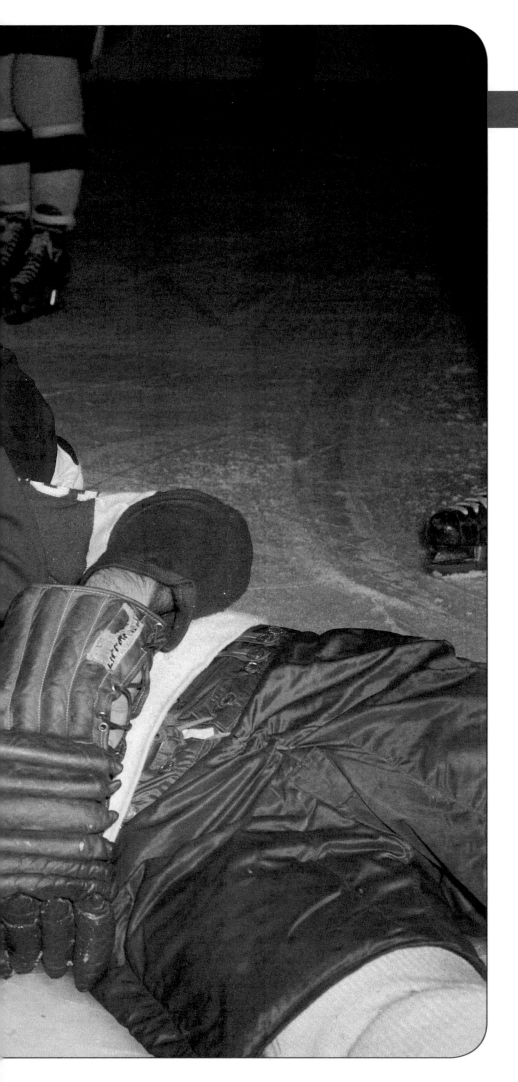

It almost came to a tragic end before any of the greatness had truly emerged.

Gordie Howe's days as a Detroit Red Wing came frighteningly close to being over at a young age.

Tommy Ivan was right in his prognosis. Howe made the jump from Omaha of the United States Hockey League right into the Red Wings lineup at the age of 18 in 1946. Detroit coach-GM Jack Adams was immediately impressed. "Here is a kid who can be as great as he shows the desire to be," Adams told Doug Vaughan of The Windsor Star. "He's got everything."

Howe wasted little time making his mark as an NHLer, beating Turk Broda in Detroit's 1946-47 season opener, a 3-3 tie with the Toronto Maple Leafs at Olympia Stadium. "It was a rebound, not much of a play," Howe remembered. "The puck just came out. I was standing in front and I flicked it in to his right, my left.

"That was about the extent of it, but I felt great. I wrote every person I knew about it."

The belligerent side of Howe came out in his second game, at Toronto against the Leafs, when he dropped the gloves and tangled with Leafs winger Bill Ezinicki, one of the NHL's toughest customers. Playing a limited role as a rookie, Howe finished with seven goals and 15 assists in 58 games, earning a combined salary and bonus figure of $12,000.

Howe improved to 12-25-37 totals as a sophomore and was enjoying a breakthrough campaign in 1948-49, moving to a regular

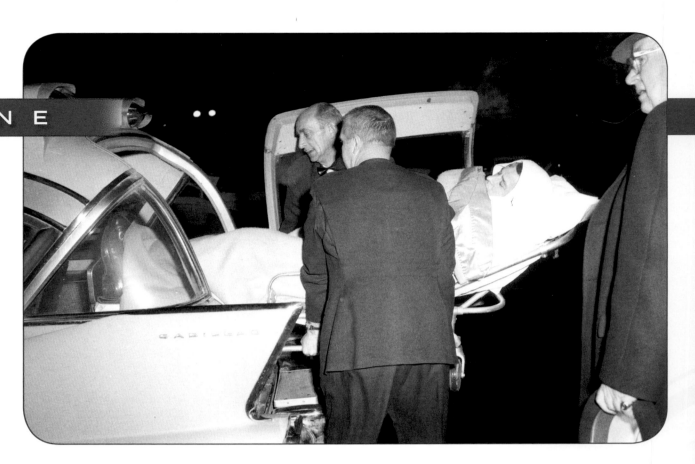

spot on Detroit's top line alongside Sid Abel and Ted Lindsay, when a knee injury scuttled much of his season. Howe underwent surgery to repair a torn ligament in his right knee and missed 20 games.

Still, he had done enough in 40 games to earn a spot on the NHL's Second All-Star Team, and it was apparent that Howe was on the brink of entering the NHL elite.

He cleared that bar the following campaign, ending up third in NHL scoring with 35 goals and

33 assists as the Wings finished atop the NHL standings for the second successive season.

A grudge-match opening-round series against Toronto -- the team that swept the Wings in the 1949 Cup final – awaited, and it didn't go well. Toronto was leading 5-0 late in Game 1 at Olympia.

Then things got much worse.

Howe went to check Toronto captain Teeder Kennedy into the boards, but Kennedy saw him at the last second and was able to spin out of the

Whatever ailment he had we would bring him in and do whatever X-ray studies on his wrists or his back. He's kind of a medical wonder, so radiologists are always excited to see his X-rays because they are unbelievable in terms of how he could tolerate the pain and continue doing what he does. His wrists are a miracle in and of themselves. He's basically got a bag of bones in both of his wrists. They're about twice the size of a normal human being's. He's had several fractures in them that were never treated at the time of the injuries so all of the bones just kind of disintegrated. When you look at the X-rays it looks like a patient that has an abnormal nervous system that doesn't detect pain. Most patients wouldn't be able to tolerate that pain.

DR. MURRAY HOWE Gordie's Son

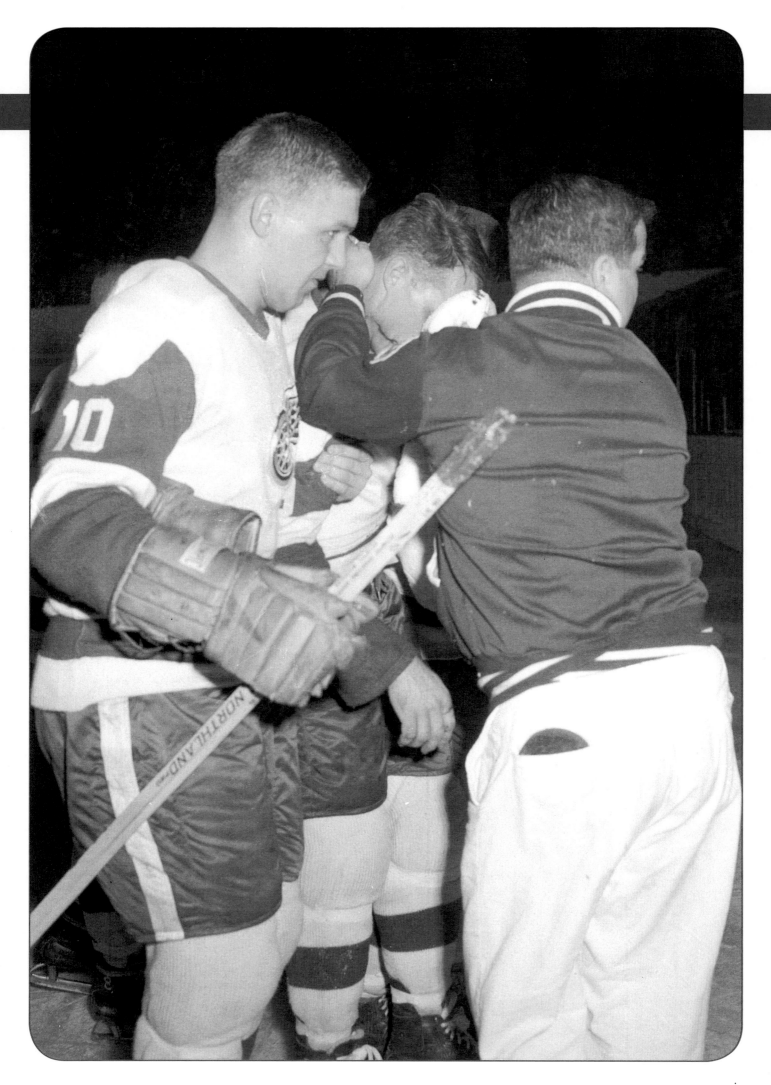

hit. Howe glanced off Kennedy and crashed hard headfirst into the boards, laying there in a motionless heap, blood quickly puddling underneath him.

"I stepped aside, and Howe crashed headlong into the boards," Kennedy told Vaughan. "I'll take an oath that to the best of my knowledge, my stick didn't touch Howe."

Howe's injuries included a fractured cheekbone, broken nose, lacerated right eyeball and severe concussion. He was vomiting blood. Carried from the ice on a stretcher, surgery was performed that night at Detroit's Harper Hospital to bore a hole through his skull and remove fluid pressure from around Howe's brain. His parents were rushed to Howe's bedside from Saskatoon in case he didn't survive the night.

"The next 24 hours will tell the story, but I think Howe will be all right," Wings team physician Dr. C.L. Tomsu told The Associated Press. "It's too early yet to judge what this will mean to Gordie's career."

Howe made an astonishing recovery. Out for the remainder of the playoffs, he watched from the sideline as the Wings won seven-game series from Toronto and the New York Rangers to win the Stanley Cup. As the celebrations began on the Olympia ice surface, fans began chanting Howe's name and he joined his teammates on the ice, his head still bandaged from his injuries.

Years later, he can joke about the memory.

"I enjoyed my first three Stanley Cups," Howe said. "I don't remember much about the first one." **9**

"We had a flock of young kids in at training camp and I couldn't take my eyes off a big rangy one. I called him over and asked his name. 'Gordon Howe', he drawled back and added, 'But I'm no relation to that other Howe over there.' I told the kid that if he worked hard, some day he might be as good as Syd Howe, one of our best forwards at the time. But honestly, I never dreamed that he'd do it."

JACK ADAMS
(in Sports Illustrated, March 18, 1957)
Coach/General Manager, 1927-63
1959 HOF Inductee

NINE

the Production Line

Hockey's most famous forward unit and their accomplishments

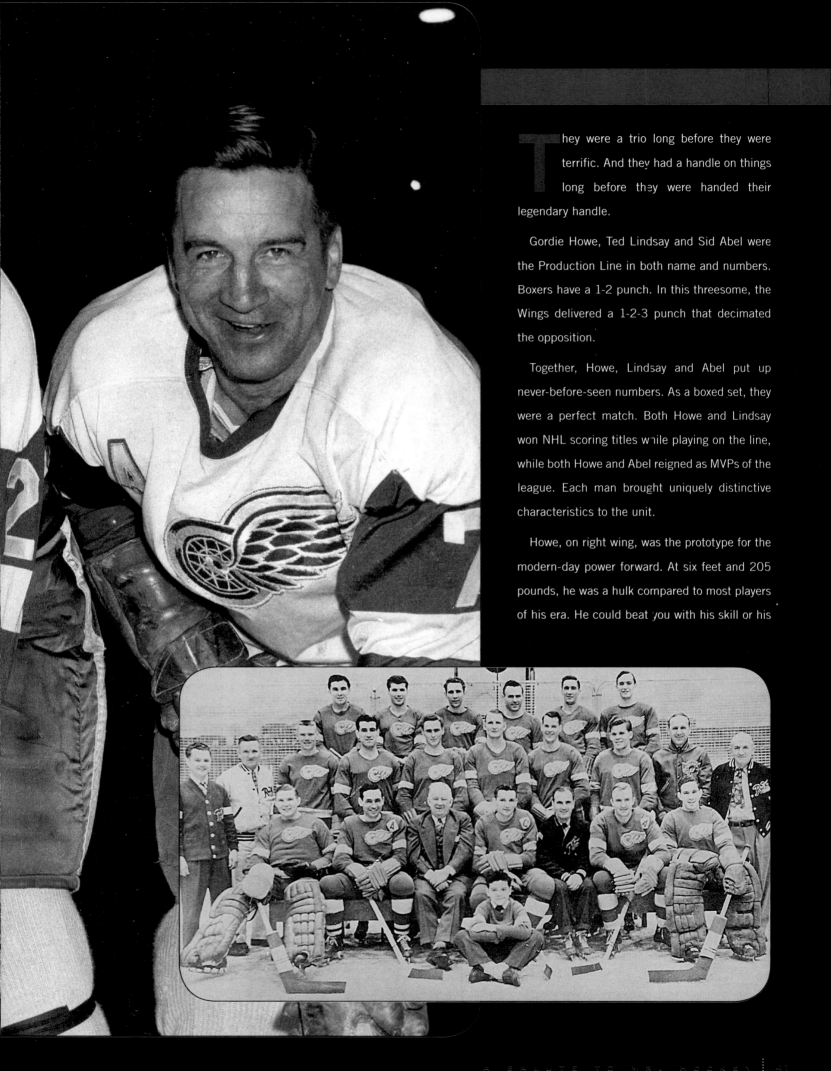

They were a trio long before they were terrific. And they had a handle on things long before they were handed their legendary handle.

Gordie Howe, Ted Lindsay and Sid Abel were the Production Line in both name and numbers. Boxers have a 1-2 punch. In this threesome, the Wings delivered a 1-2-3 punch that decimated the opposition.

Together, Howe, Lindsay and Abel put up never-before-seen numbers. As a boxed set, they were a perfect match. Both Howe and Lindsay won NHL scoring titles while playing on the line, while both Howe and Abel reigned as MVPs of the league. Each man brought uniquely distinctive characteristics to the unit.

Howe, on right wing, was the prototype for the modern-day power forward. At six feet and 205 pounds, he was a hulk compared to most players of his era. He could beat you with his skill or his

size and eschewed the slapshot for the wrist shot feeling its quick release offered more potential to catch a netminder napping. Howe policed his area of the ice, and anyone foolhardy enough to cross him lived to regret that decision.

Left-winger Lindsay was the epitome of the non-conformist, a man who stood his ground and stood up for his beliefs. Someone who absolutely detested losing, he played the game like a Tasmanian Devil on skates and despite his seemingly slight five-foot-eight, 163-pound frame, was one of the NHL's most feared opponents and perhaps the most hated opposing player in the history of the game.

"He's the guy who holds us together," Abel once said of Lindsay. "He keeps us at a high pitch."

Abel, the center, was the veteran of the group, coming to Detroit a decade before the glory days of the unit. By the time the Production Line was humming, he'd already captained Detroit to one Stanley Cup and would guide them to two more flanked by his fellow all-star wingers.

Gordie was the greatest player of my time. I had to be on my toes because he had a great shot and skated with two great players in Sid Abel and Ted Lindsay. I had to watch him all of the time when he came down the ice. He was outstanding. One thing that I remember about Gordie Howe was his energy. If he just finished a shift on the ice and they got a penalty, he would come right back and help kill the penalty. He had a lot of endurance.

"He was strong and he could defend himself very well. He wasn't a fighter, but we knew that he was strong. The fans appreciated him because they compared him to the Rocket Richard. For me, Gordie was just as good as the Rocket.

EMILE BOUCHARD | Defenseman, 1941-56
1966 HOF Inductee

He was the best hockey player I'd ever seen. He did everything well. He was good offensively; he was good defensively. And in those days, you had to fight your own battles, and he could do that job too. No one bothered him too much.

"We all had talent. Sid was our father. We were his young legs; we could cover more ice than he could at the time. It was a good association. We all knew what each other were doing on the ice, and that's why it worked out so good."

TED LINDSAY | Left wing, 1944-65
1966 HOF Inductee

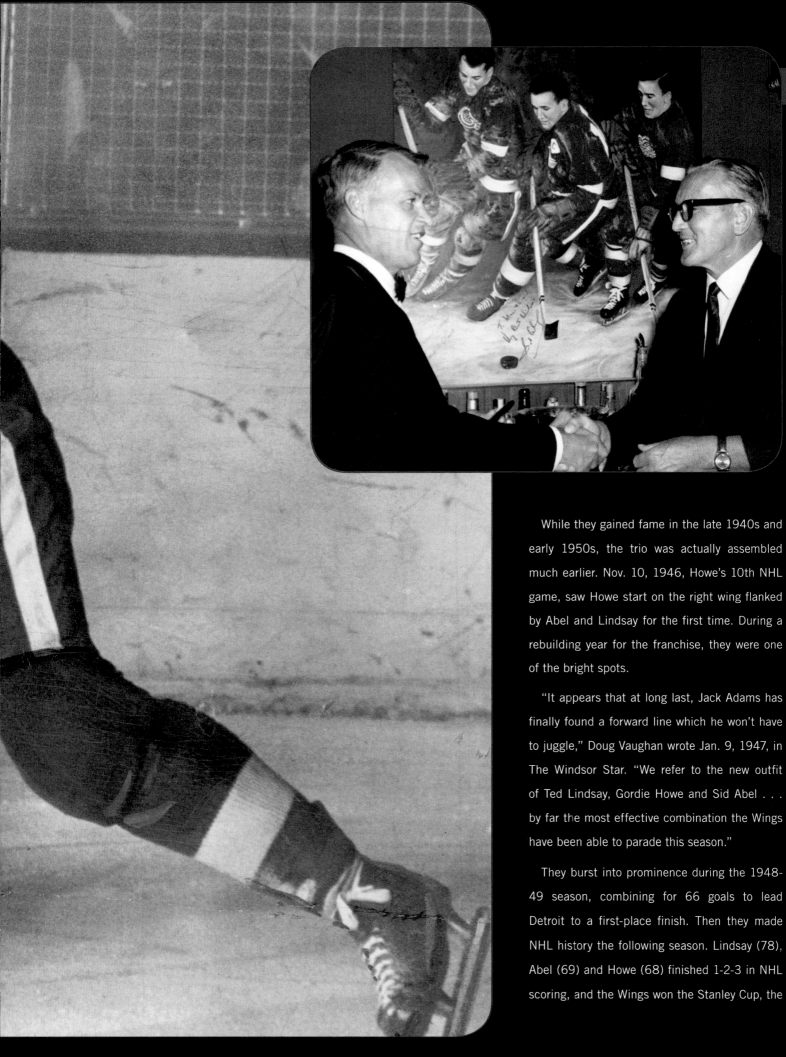

While they gained fame in the late 1940s and early 1950s, the trio was actually assembled much earlier. Nov. 10, 1946, Howe's 10th NHL game, saw Howe start on the right wing flanked by Abel and Lindsay for the first time. During a rebuilding year for the franchise, they were one of the bright spots.

"It appears that at long last, Jack Adams has finally found a forward line which he won't have to juggle," Doug Vaughan wrote Jan. 9, 1947, in The Windsor Star. "We refer to the new outfit of Ted Lindsay, Gordie Howe and Sid Abel . . . by far the most effective combination the Wings have been able to parade this season."

They burst into prominence during the 1948-49 season, combining for 66 goals to lead Detroit to a first-place finish. Then they made NHL history the following season. Lindsay (78), Abel (69) and Howe (68) finished 1-2-3 in NHL scoring, and the Wings won the Stanley Cup, the

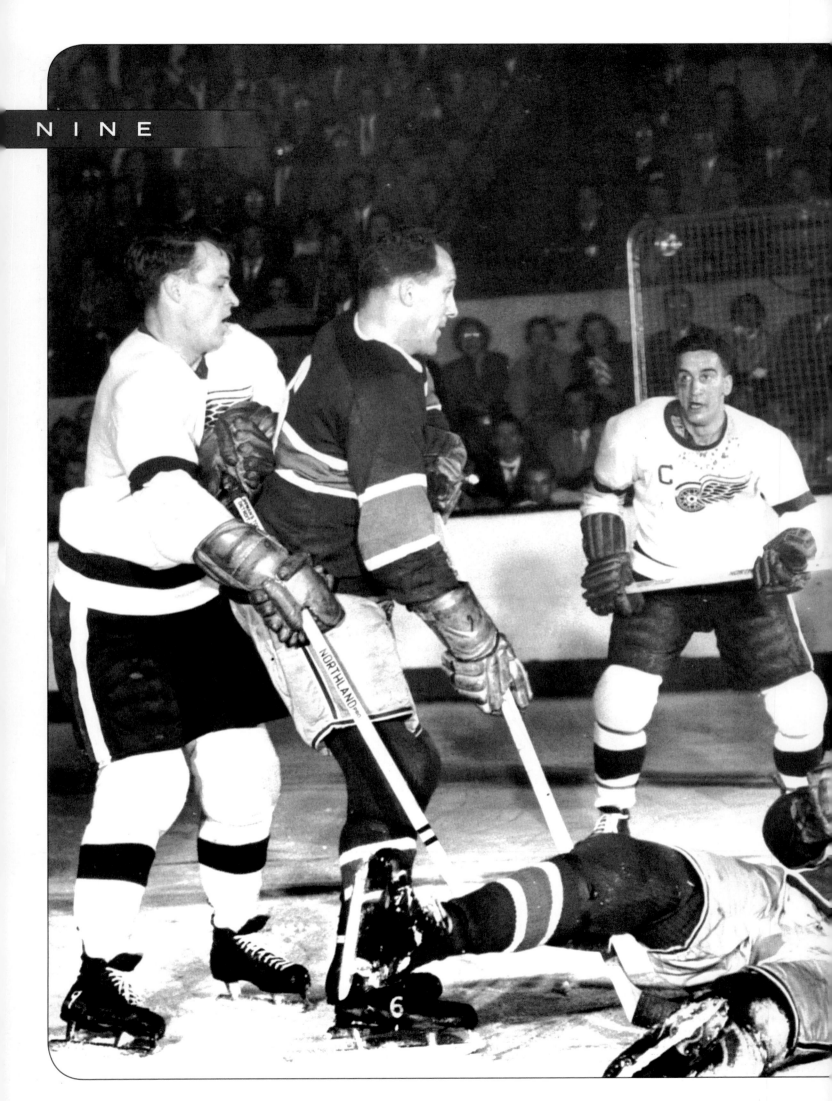

SPORTS ILLUSTRATED

MARCH 18, 1957
a Time Inc. weekly publication

25 CENTS
$7.50 A YEAR

THE SECOND LESSON BY BEN HOGAN

LINDSAY AND HOWE
RED-HOT RED WINGS

THE PUCK HAS EYES

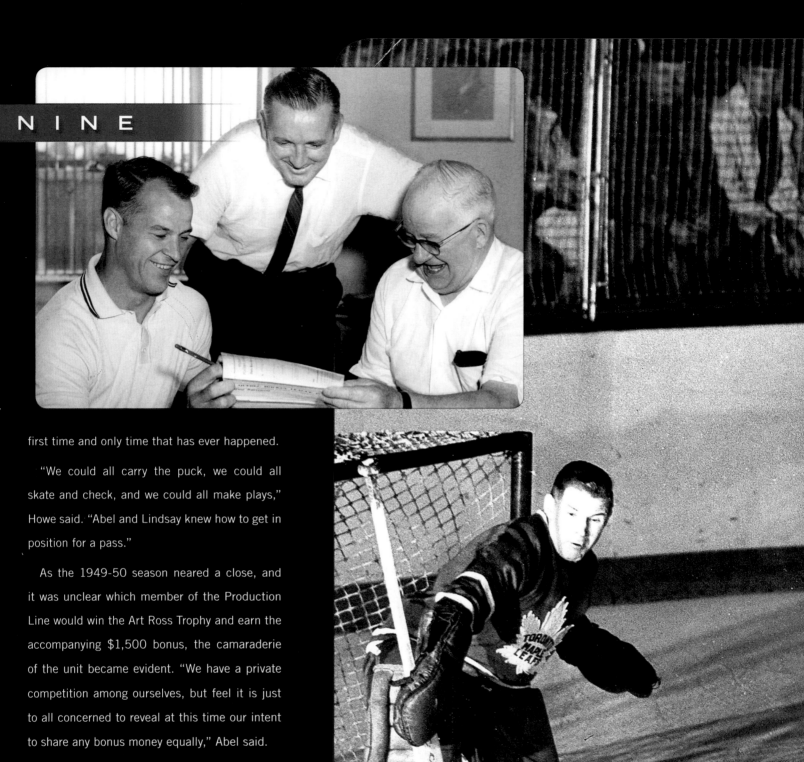

first time and only time that has ever happened.

"We could all carry the puck, we could all skate and check, and we could all make plays," Howe said. "Abel and Lindsay knew how to get in position for a pass."

As the 1949-50 season neared a close, and it was unclear which member of the Production Line would win the Art Ross Trophy and earn the accompanying $1,500 bonus, the camaraderie of the unit became evident. "We have a private competition among ourselves, but feel it is just to all concerned to reveal at this time our intent to share any bonus money equally," Abel said.

As a unit, all three members figured in a goal together 60 times. While they clearly made a name for themselves, naming them was late in arriving. The line was given the unsexy handles of the Abel Line and the Big Line, until finally, early in the 1950-51 season, Adams appropriately christened them.

"This is the Motor City of hockey, so the Production Line sounds like a good name," Adams said.

The unit was officially dissolved in 1952, when Abel accepted a position as head coach of the Chicago Blackhawks.

Howe (No. 9, March 12, 1972), Lindsay (No. 7, Nov. 10, 1991) and Abel (No. 12, Apr. 29, 1995) were all granted permanent legacy with the team when their numbers were retired.

"To go up there between my old buddies Gordie (Howe) and Ted (Lindsay) again is a very touching moment," Abel said when his sweater joined the other two and was hung from the Joe Louis Arena rafters.

Fitting recognition for three legends of Hockeytown. **9**

Detroit Red Wings 1949-50

James Norris (pres) James D Norris (v pres)
Art M Wirtz (sec treas) Jack Adams manager
Tom Ivan coach   Fred A Huber jr (pub direct)
Carson Cooper head scout   C Mattson trainer
W Humeniuk ass't train Sid Abel captain

Pete Babando	Clare Martin	James McFadden
Steve Black	Max McNab	Joe Carveth
G Couture	Marty Pavelich	Al Dewsbury
Jimmy Peters	Lee Fogolin	M Pronovost
George Gee	Leo Reise	Gordon Howe
Red Kelly	Jack Stewart	Ted Lindsey
John Wilson	Harry Lumley	Larry Wilson

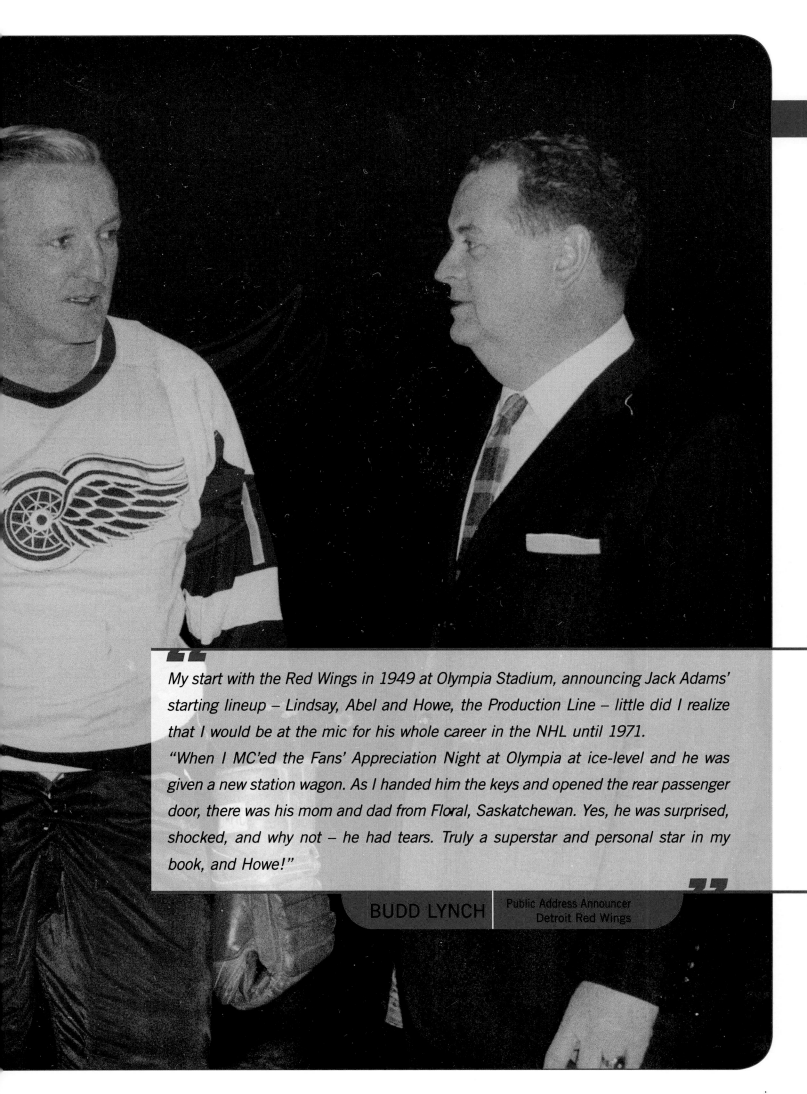

My start with the Red Wings in 1949 at Olympia Stadium, announcing Jack Adams'
starting lineup – Lindsay, Abel and Howe, the Production Line – little did I realize
that I would be at the mic for his whole career in the NHL until 1971.

"When I MC'ed the Fans' Appreciation Night at Olympia at ice-level and he was
given a new station wagon. As I handed him the keys and opened the rear passenger
door, there was his mom and dad from Floral, Saskatchewan. Yes, he was surprised,
shocked, and why not – he had tears. Truly a superstar and personal star in my
book, and Howe!"

BUDD LYNCH | Public Address Announcer
Detroit Red Wings

LINDSAY 7
1944-1957
1964-1965

ABEL 12
1938-1943
1945-1952

HOWE 9
1946-1971

NINE

the Glory Days

With Howe leading the way, Detroit won four Stanley Cups

First, they worried about whether Gordie Howe would survive. Then, they wondered whether he'd ever play the game again.

Turns out there was nothing to worry about - unless you were part of the opposing team that was supposed to stop Howe.

He returned for the 1950-51 season from the devastating head injury he suffered in the 1950 playoffs and gave everyone else in the National Hockey League a headache, one that would last for the next two decades and that no pain reliever was capable of subsiding.

Howe was about to take a wrecking ball to the NHL record book and take the Red Wings to the top of the league.

Already, there were back-to-back first-place finishes and one Stanley Cup title on the resume when that 1950-51 campaign got underway, but much more was on the way. Wearing a helmet on occasion to combat the headaches and dizziness that were sporadic side-effects of the severe concussion he suffered the previous spring, there was no stopping Howe.

"*He was tough because he could shoot with either hand, so it made him hard to contain, he was hard to stop. You could never relax when he was on the ice, because he would turn you inside-out, and the next thing you'd know, you were digging the puck out of your net. I'm sure he did it to me a few times, but he did it to everybody.*

"*He's been a great model for the young players of today. He was so great and he could do things so well. Everything came natural to him. He was a super guy.*"

LEO BOIVIN Defenseman, 1951-70
1986 HOF Inductee

He charged to the NHL scoring title and with 86 points and won his first Art Ross Trophy, shattering the previous NHL point mark of 82 that was set by Boston's Herb Cain in 1943-44.

He was establishing his credentials as the NHL's most dominant player. The heir to the throne held by Montreal's Maurice (Rocket) Richard showcased his abilities as they honored the Rocket on Feb. 17, 1950, at the Montreal Forum, setting up a goal and scoring the winner in Detroit's 2-1 victory on 'Rocket Richard' night.

Even the Rocket himself had to admit there was a new sheriff in town. "Howe was a better all-around player than I was," Richard said. "He could do everything."

Everything and then some.

He was the best player on the league's best team. Howe won another Art Ross Trophy in 1951-52, tying his mark of 86 points as Detroit won the Stanley Cup in the minimum eight games required. He also captured the first of five Hart Trophies as league MVP.

The following season, he was MVP again, establishing a new league points mark of 95, becoming the first NHLer to ascend to and beyond the 90-point plateau. Howe's 49 goals set a Detroit club mark that stood for two decades.

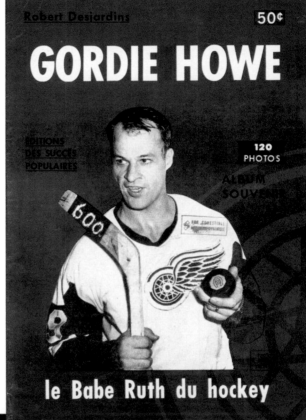

Robert Desjardins — 50¢

GORDIE HOWE

ÉDITIONS DES SUCCÈS POPULAIRES — 120 PHOTOS — ALBUM SOUVENIR

le Babe Ruth du hockey

N I N E

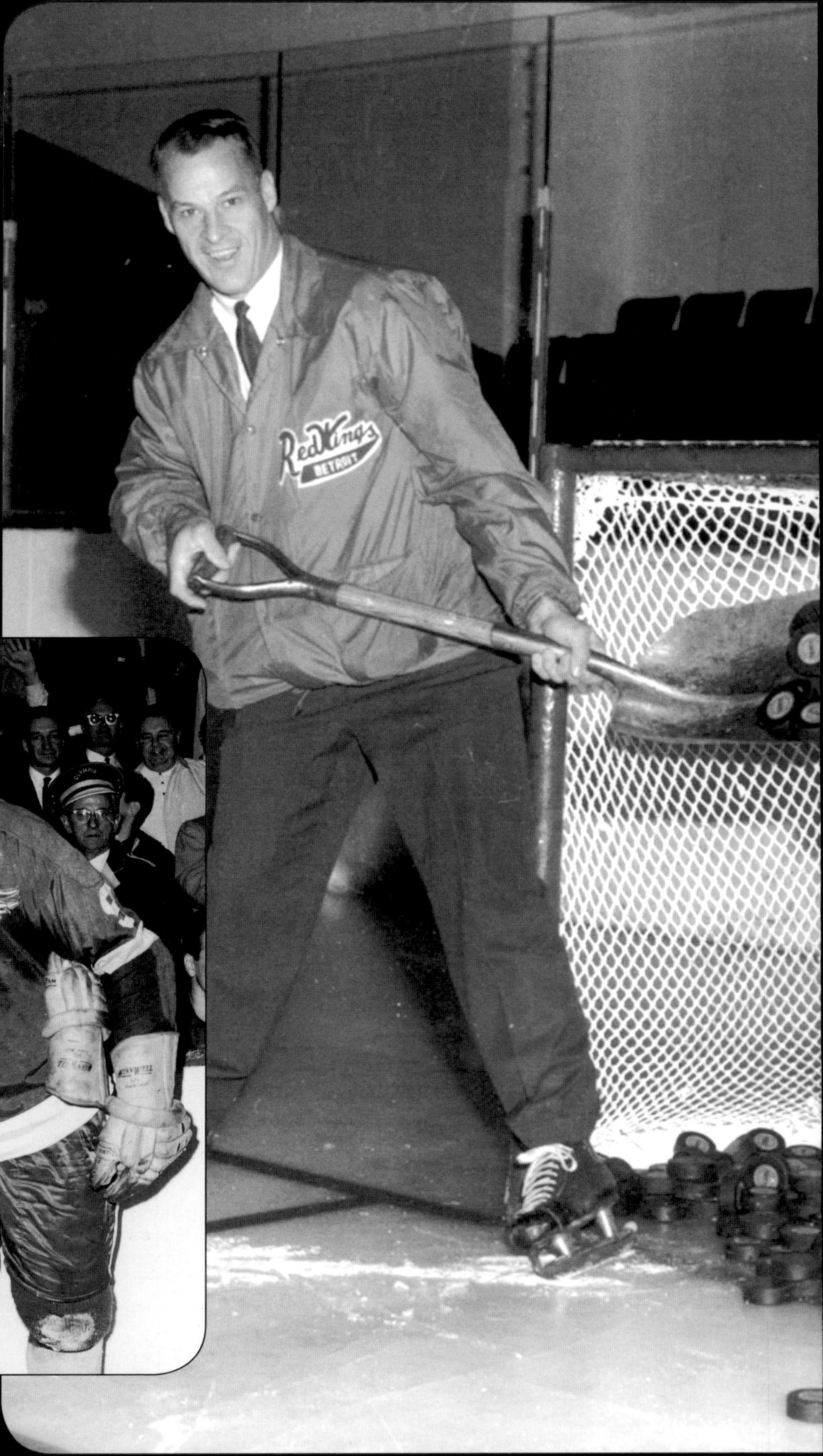

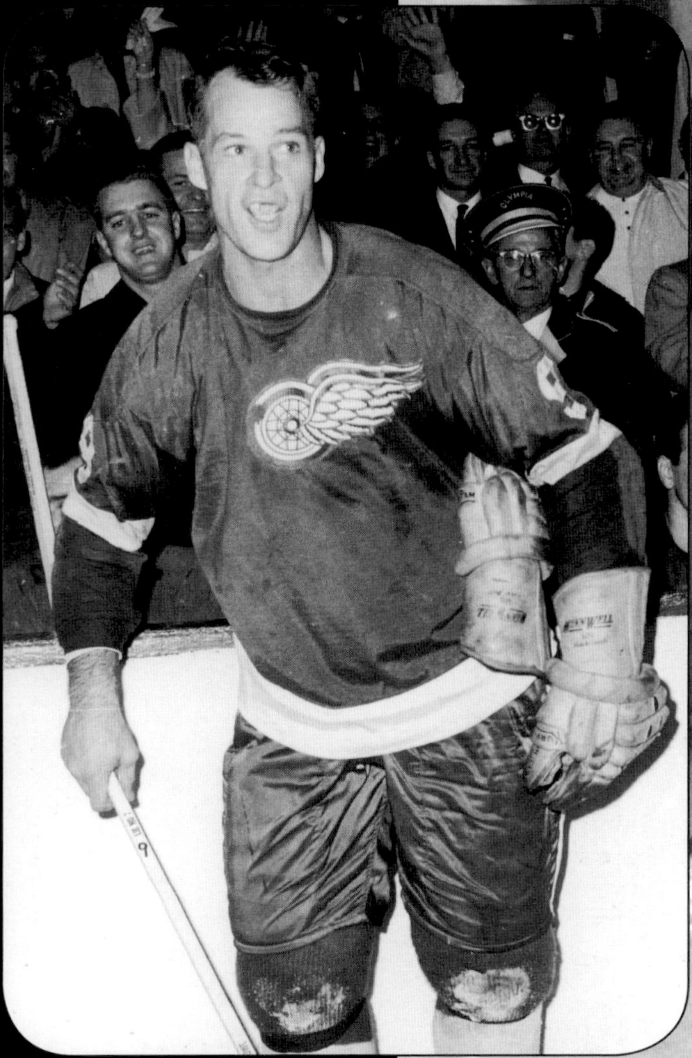

November 10, 1963—Gordie Howe attains a new pedestal, in a career of high achievement, as he scores record-breaking 545th National Hockey League goal.

Painted by Jacques Tremblay, R.I. in the Prudential Collection "Great Moments in Canadian Sport".

"He gets so many goals, he just counts them in bunches," teammate Marty Pavelich said of Howe.

A club-record 48 assists and a fourth consecutive league scoring title followed in 1953-54, as did another Stanley Cup title. The next season brought a fourth Stanley Cup and Howe's most dominating playoff performance. His 20 post-season points were a league record that stood until 1970, and a Red Wings' mark that held forth until 1988.

"Those teams had a little bit of everything," former Detroit forward Bill Dineen said. "We had talent with guys like Howe and (Red) Kelly, we had a great goalie in (Terry) Sawchuk, we had toughness -- nobody wanted to mess with Howe and (Ted) Lindsay, and (Marcel) Pronovost was a great hitter. And guys like (Glen) Skov and Pavelich and (Tony) Leswick were great checkers."

Howe fondly remember the closeness of those Wings teams. "After games, we always went somewhere together," he said.

By now, the Howe talk was turning from greatest of his era to the best of all-time. "There's no denying that Richard was a great scorer, but common sense will tell anyone that Howe is the finest, most complete hockey player in the history of the game," Detroit GM Jack Adams expressed. "He does all things and does all of them better than anyone else."

Even Howe's opponents were delivering the superlatives.

"Nobody ever could do or did the things on the ice that he did," said former NHL goalie and longtime league executive Emile Francis, a victim of 10 Howe goals. "Gordie gets my vote as the best ever." **9**

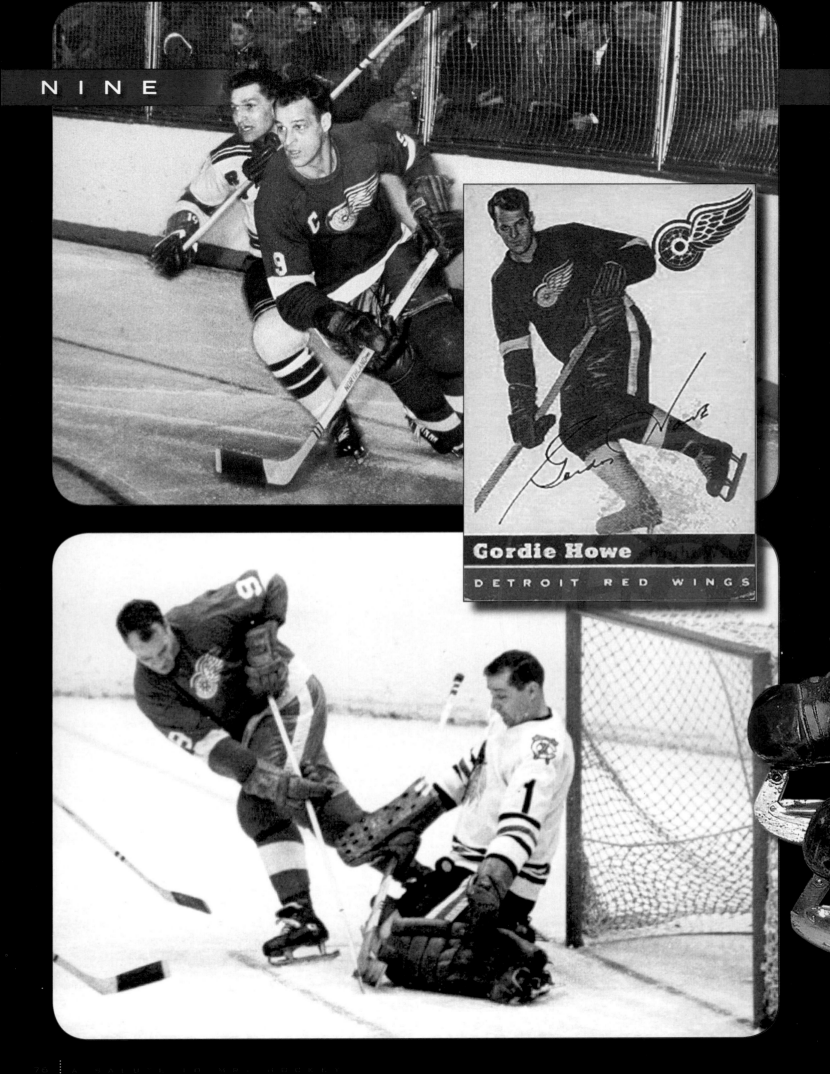

Gordie Howe Right Wing
DETROIT RED WINGS

"He was a guy who was offensively stellar, defensively sound. He played hardnosed; he was mean. As a Canadian kid, you were brought up to go out there and play hard, be offensive, and be on the ice in all key situations.

"He set the tone for what a Canadian hockey player should be. How hard he played on the ice, how skilled he was, how tough he was and what a gentleman he was off the ice. What he showed was how you can be a great player and still be humble. There are very few players like that. Bobby Orr is like that. They were unbelievable players but still had that humility about them.

"I played with his son Marty. He was my defense partner in Boston the year before I came to Detroit. I broke in Steve Yzerman. You'd have to say Gordie, Ted Lindsay and Steve Yzerman — those are the guys that epitomize the Detroit Red Wings."

BRAD PARK | Defenseman, 1968-85
1988 HOF Inductee

Milestone Goals

1st Goal	Oct. 16, 1946	vs. Toronto
100th Goal	Mar. 15, 1950	vs. Montreal
200th Goal	Feb. 15, 1953	vs. Chicago
300th Goal	Feb. 7, 1956	vs. Chicago
400th Goal	Dec. 13, 1958	vs. Montreal
500th Goal	Mar. 14, 1962	vs. NY Rangers
544th Goal	Oct. 27, 1963	vs. Montreal*
545th Goal	Nov. 10, 1963	vs. Montreal**
600th Goal	Nov. 27, 1965	vs. Montreal
700th Goal	Dec. 4, 1968	vs. Pittsburgh
786th Goal	Apr. 3, 1971	vs. Chicago***
801st Goal	Apr. 6, 1980	vs. Detroit

* *Tied Maurice (Rocket) Richard for all-time NHL lead*
** *Surpassed Maurice (Rocket) Richard for all-time NHL lead*
*** *Final regular-season goal as a Red Wing*

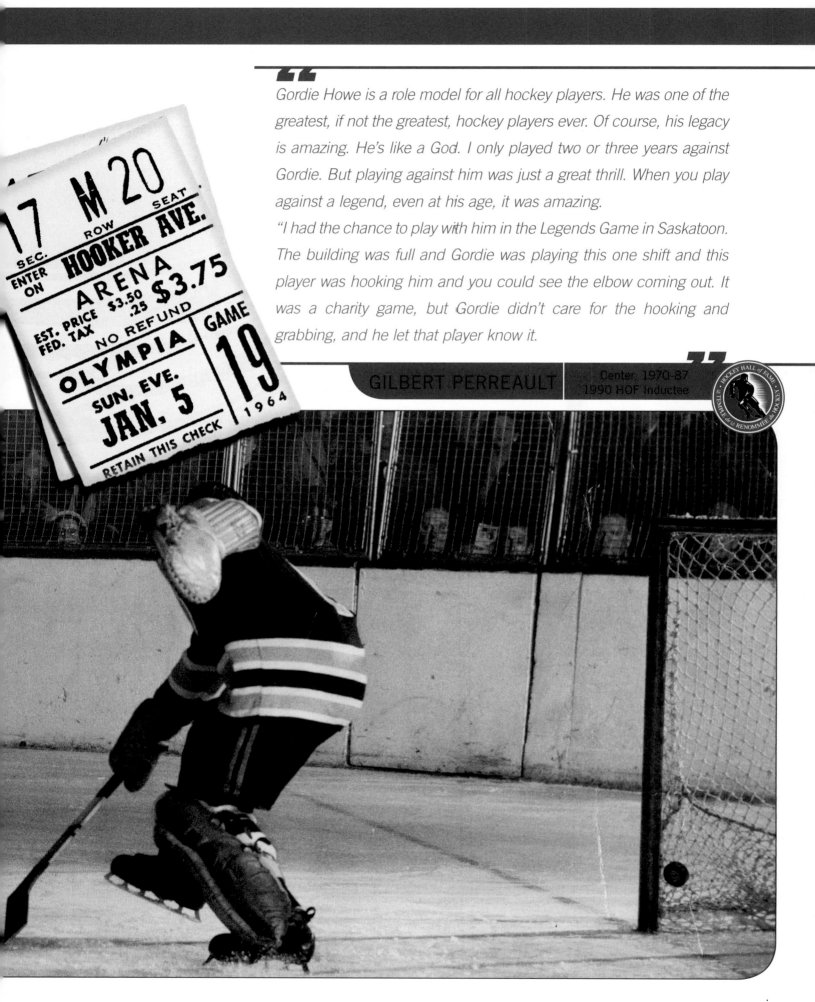

Gordie Howe is a role model for all hockey players. He was one of the greatest, if not the greatest, hockey players ever. Of course, his legacy is amazing. He's like a God. I only played two or three years against Gordie. But playing against him was just a great thrill. When you play against a legend, even at his age, it was amazing.

"I had the chance to play with him in the Legends Game in Saskatoon. The building was full and Gordie was playing this one shift and this player was hooking him and you could see the elbow coming out. It was a charity game, but Gordie didn't care for the hooking and grabbing, and he let that player know it.

GILBERT PERREAULT | Center, 1970-87
1990 HOF Inductee

NINE

the Making of Mr. Hockey

While rewriting the record book,
Howe evolved into hockey's
greatest ambassador

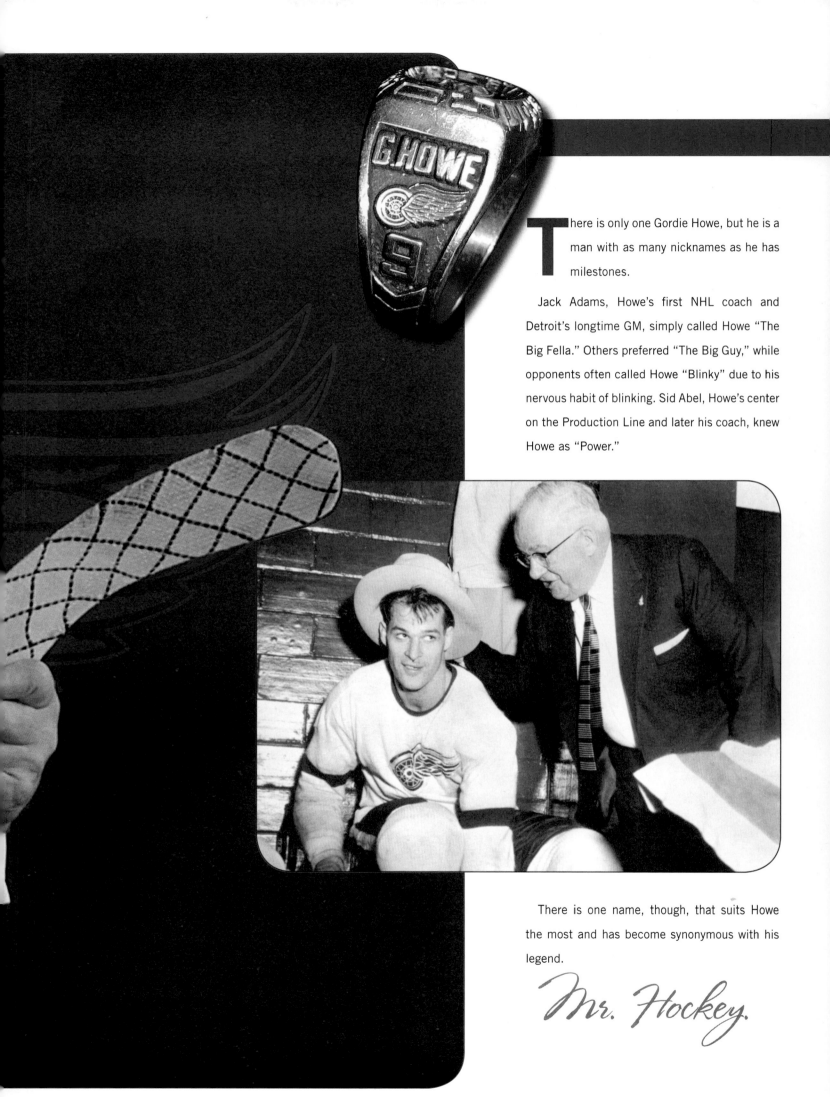

There is only one Gordie Howe, but he is a man with as many nicknames as he has milestones.

Jack Adams, Howe's first NHL coach and Detroit's longtime GM, simply called Howe "The Big Fella." Others preferred "The Big Guy," while opponents often called Howe "Blinky" due to his nervous habit of blinking. Sid Abel, Howe's center on the Production Line and later his coach, knew Howe as "Power."

There is one name, though, that suits Howe the most and has become synonymous with his legend.

Mr. Hockey.

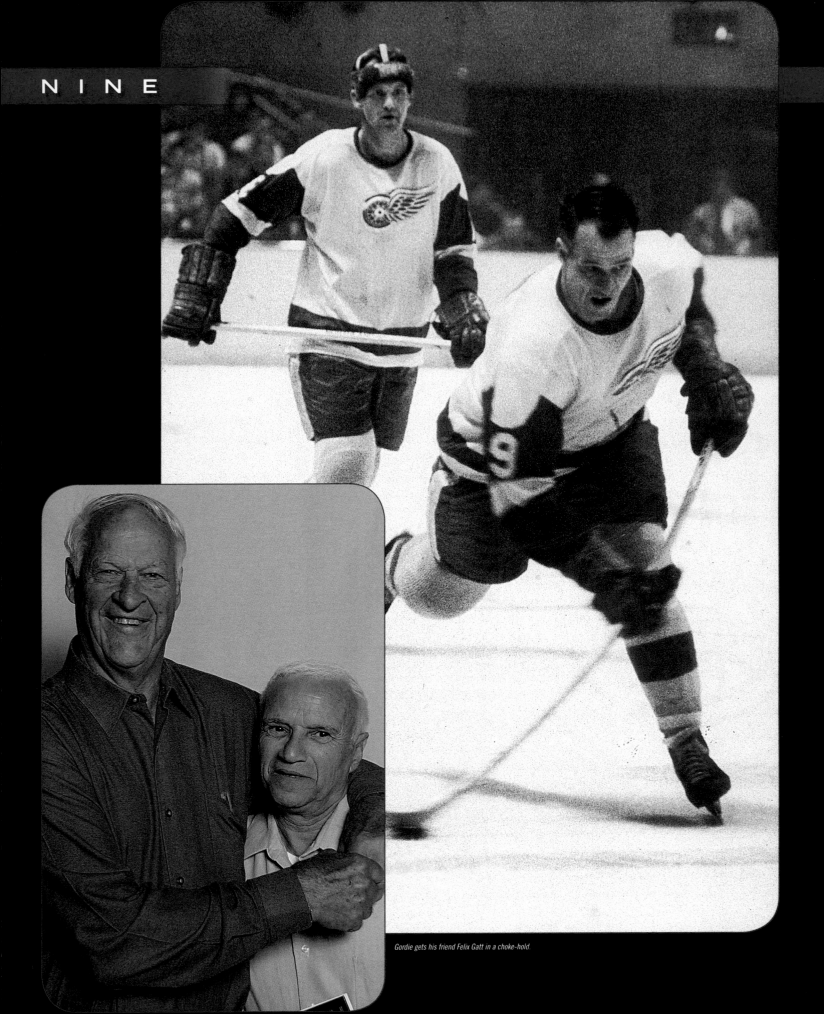

Gordie gets his friend Felix Gatt in a choke-hold.

GORDIE HOWE
"MR. HOCKEY"

LARS
FLOWERS

"Many people have tried to start a feud between us, they say I don't like Howe. It's not true. He is a great hockey player. If I had to make any comment about the guy it would be that he doesn't seem to go all out every time he's out there. If he did, there's no telling what he might do to the record book."

MAURICE (ROCKET) RICHARD
(in Sports Illustrated, March 18, 1957)
Right wing, 1942-60
1961 HOF Inductee

"I was asked to speak at a Lions Club dinner when I was 10, and Gordie Howe was going to be one of the guest speakers, and I was going to sit at the head table. I was all excited to be a part of it and get the chance to meet Gordie Howe. This is when the infamous picture of him and I was taken. When you're a kid and you look up to somebody and he becomes your hero and then your mentor, a lot of times kids get disappointed. For me when I met Gordie Howe I always remember telling my dad that he was bigger and better than I had ever imagined. He was genuinely a nice man and obviously the greatest player that ever played. So for me I was really lucky that my idol was as nice as he was.

"I was tongue-tied for hours. He was the greatest person for me to meet because he taught me about being humble and about being nice to people. Gordie Howe never blew anybody off ever in his life. He was always genuinely nice to each and every person who ever came over to him, and signing autographs and taking pictures. At that time I think he was 38-years-old and if he could be doing that at that age, it couldn't be that hard for everybody to sign autographs and take pictures, so those were valuable lessons for me."

WAYNE GRETZKY | Center, 1979-99
1999 HOF Inductee

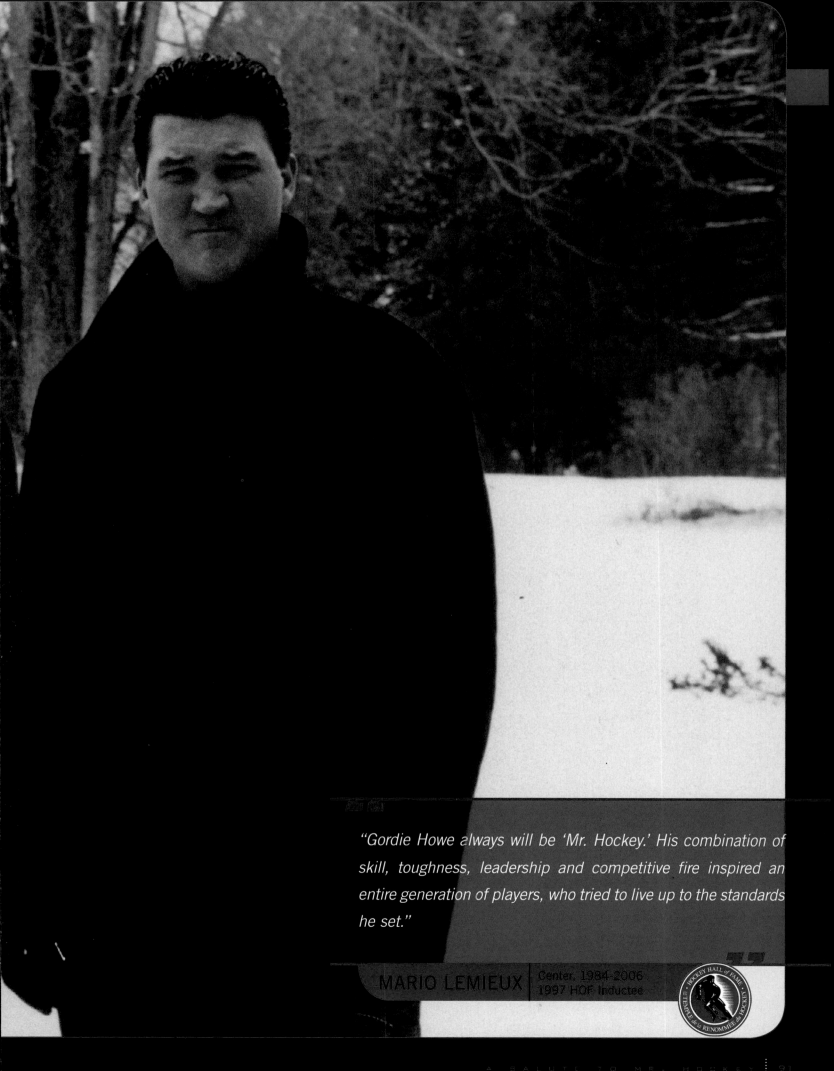

"Gordie Howe always will be 'Mr. Hockey.' His combination of skill, toughness, leadership and competitive fire inspired an entire generation of players, who tried to live up to the standards he set."

MARIO LEMIEUX | Center, 1984-2006
1997 HOF Inductee

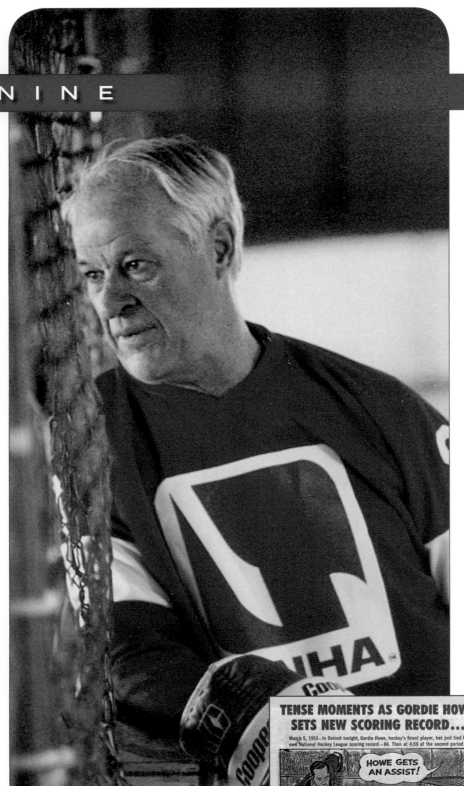

It succinctly explains who he is and what he is all about, not to mention the reverence in which he is held by the general public.

The name was bestowed on Howe by another hockey legend. Before Howe, before the Rocket, the game's greatest goal scorer was a man they called "Old Poison." Nels Stewart authored 324 NHL goals and is generally given credit for supplying Howe with his famous moniker.

Stewart was speaking at a banquet in Toronto late in the 1952-53 NHL season. Montreal's Maurice (Rocket) Richard had recently surpassed Stewart as the NHL's career scoring leader, but Stewart noted it was likely that Richard was only renting the space. "Another Mr. Hockey in the person of Gordie Howe will pass both of us one of these days," Stewart remarked.

How right he was.

Over the span of his career, Howe broke more records than were exploded in Chicago on Disco Demolition Night.

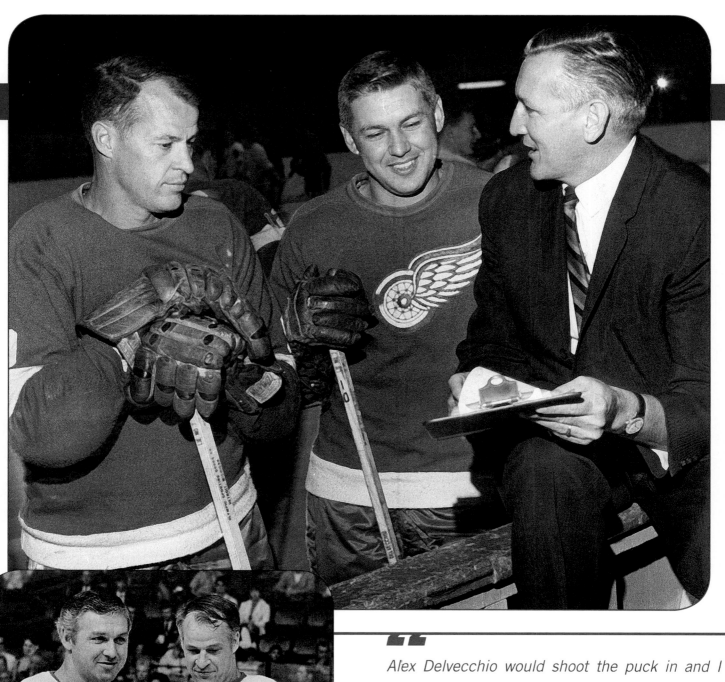

> Alex Delvecchio would shoot the puck in and I would go out and shoot it back over the blue line. Good old Gordie said, 'You're going to do that one too many.' The next time it was fired into the left corner I went out and got it, and the next thing I knew I was laying on the ice and old Mr. Elbows got me. I was down on the ice and he skated over and said, 'I told you so.' I'll never forget that. I was never worried who had the puck. I was always worried about, 'Where is No. 9? Where is he on the ice?'

EDDIE GIACOMIN | Goalie, 1959-78
1987 HOF Inductee

NINE

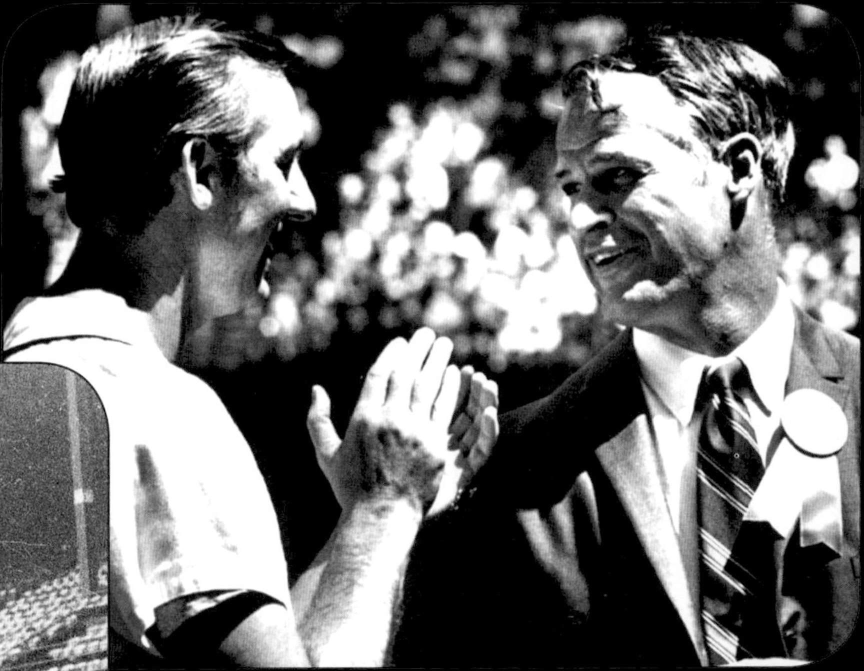

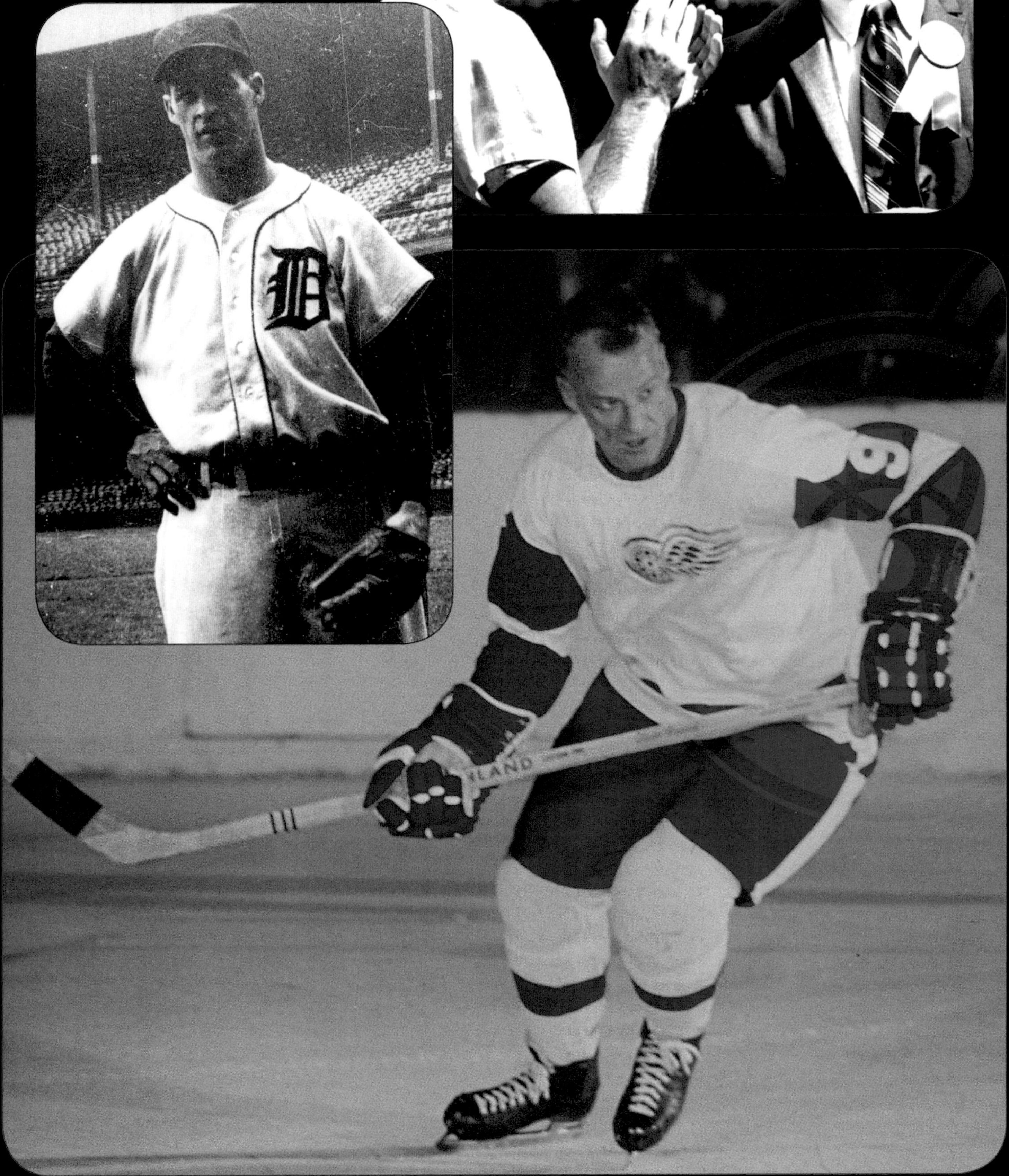

from 26-34 minutes per night of ice time. One game against Montreal during the 1960-61 season, Howe skated nearly 45 minutes of ice time. He double shifted, killed penalties, worked the power play and even took turns on defense. "We haven't tried him in goal yet," Adams joked.

Howe was also the toughest customer on the ice. "He's got more elbows than an octopus," Selke said. "If an octopus has elbows."

Players learned to keep their distance from Howe, and those who didn't lived to regret the decision. In his most famous bout on Feb. 1, 1959, Howe destroyed the reputation and face of New York Rangers defenseman Lou Fontinato, considered the NHL's best fighter at the time, leaving Fontinato's nose badly broken and listing toward his right ear. "Louie's a funny game," said Dean Prentice, a Ranger that night, but later Howe's teammate in Detroit. "He thinks he won that fight."

With an assist against Toronto on Jan. 16, 1960, Howe moved past Richard (945 points) and became the NHL's career scoring leader. Another helper against the Leafs on Nov. 27, 1960, made Howe the first 1,000-point scorer in NHL history. That spring, he surpassed Doug Harvey to take over as the NHL's all-time playoff scoring leader. Finally, on Nov. 10, 1963, while killing a penalty during a 3-0 win over the Canadiens, Howe beat Montreal goalie Charlie Hodge for goal No. 545, once more surpassing the Rocket's NHL mark.

Now, all of the league's career standards belonged to Howe, as did the appropriate accolades. "I've been watching the game as a fan and official since the early 1900s," Montreal GM Frank Selke said in a 1961 Canadian Press interview. "I've never seen anyone combine so many faculties. He's simply the greatest."

It was more than numbers with Howe. It was also about strength, stamina and endurance. In a game against New York during the 1950s, Howe personally outshot the Rangers 18-17. He played 25 seasons as a Red Wing and logged anywhere

Howe's aura has grown to a point where he transcends the sport, and even today, nearly three decades after his final NHL game, he's still hockey's most recognizable face and its greatest ambassador.

He receives fan mail from around the globe. One such letter was addressed as follows: To Gordie Howe (The Great Hockey Player), Wherever He May Be, Either U.S. or Canada."

The letter reached its destination.

It's no surprise. As former Wing Adam Graves once remarked, "There's only one Mr. Hockey." **9**

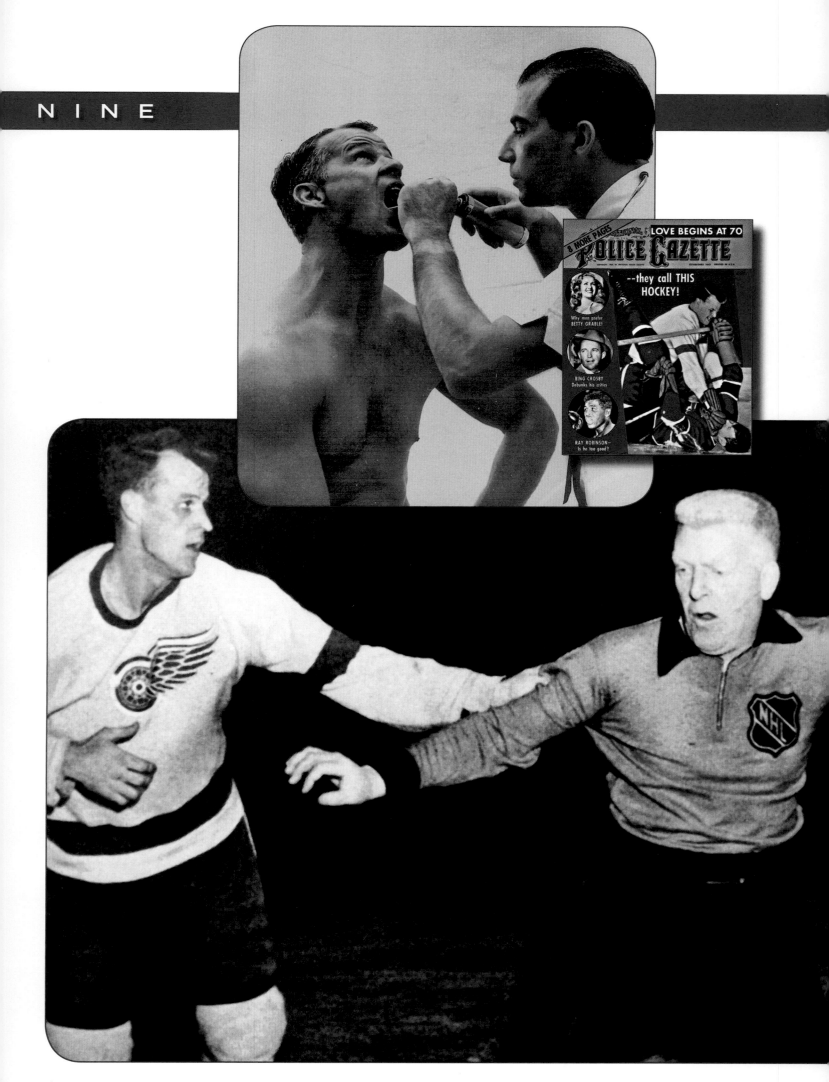

POLICE GAZETTE

8 MORE PAGES

LOVE BEGINS AT 70

--they call THIS HOCKEY!

Why men prefer BETTY GRABLE!

BING CROSBY Debunks his critics

RAY ROBINSON— Is he too good?

> "You were never going to knock Gordie off his skates because he was too strong of a skater, he was a big guy. If I tried to knock him down, he'd bounce off of me, skate around and score a goal. Going against somebody like that -- you couldn't keep them from doing things – all you could do was keep them to the board-side, the furthest from the net and at a bad angle. If we were playing against Gordie, we would tell Johnny Bower that we'll keep him at a bad angle against the boards, and if you can't stop him from there, we're going to get a new goaltender."

ALLAN STANLEY | Defenseman, 1948-69
1981 HOF Inductee

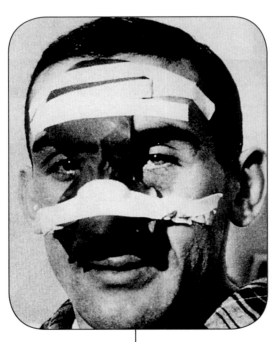

DON'T MESS AROUND WITH GORDIE

Hockey's tough guy discovers that game's best player is a rough man in a fight

Gordie Howe and Lou Fontinato are puck pushers by trade, not pugilists. But during a New York Rangers-Detroit Red Wings hockey game at Madison Square Garden last week they interrupted their stickwork for a brief, bloody battle and wound up - especially Fontinato - looking as if they'd just been through a tough ten-rounder.

The fight, which teammates called the fiercest in years, started when the Rangers' Fontinato, self-appointed tough guy of the league, was aroused by the rough treatment Howe was dishing out to one of Lou's teammates He threw down his gloves and went for Gordie. "There was nothing I could do but fight," said Howe. For a full minute the two whaled away behind the cage. The officials left them alone as the game stopped and fellow players gathered to watch. "Howe's punches went whop-whop-whop," remarked a teammate, "just like someone chopping wood."

When the two players were finally separated, it was more than clear that Howe had gotten the best of things. Lou was bloodied and his nose was broken for the fifth time in his hot-tempered career. In the hospital, after the nose was hammered back into shape, he was still full of fight. "Howe needn't think he's Jack Dempsey just because he put me here." Howe who is the best all-round player in hockey, paid no attention to the taunt. "I come to play hockey," he remarked mildly, "not to fight."

When I was a kid I received a Red Wings outfit for Christmas. At that time, Gordie and Ted Lindsay and Sid Abel were the best line, so I became a big fan of the Red Wings. When I was traded to Detroit and my brother (Pete) was already there, it was the best scenario for me having been a Red Wings' fan growing up.

"He was such a great leader. He brought things up to a certain level and everybody followed. He gave me confidence. He made you feel part of the team, even when a rookie came in he would support the younger players. You'll never see a player like him again with the sloped shoulders, the way he skated and his balance. He's one of the greatest athletes that the world has ever known.

FRANK MAHOVLICH | Left winger, 1956-78
1981 HOF Inductee

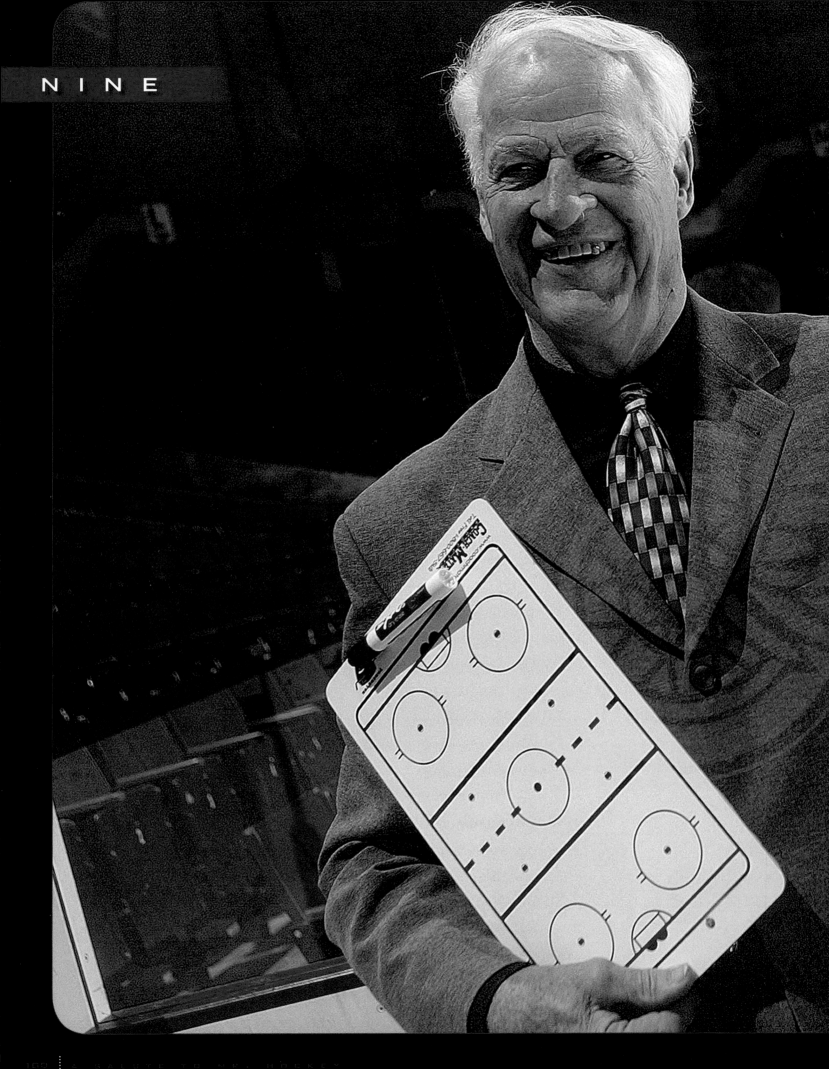

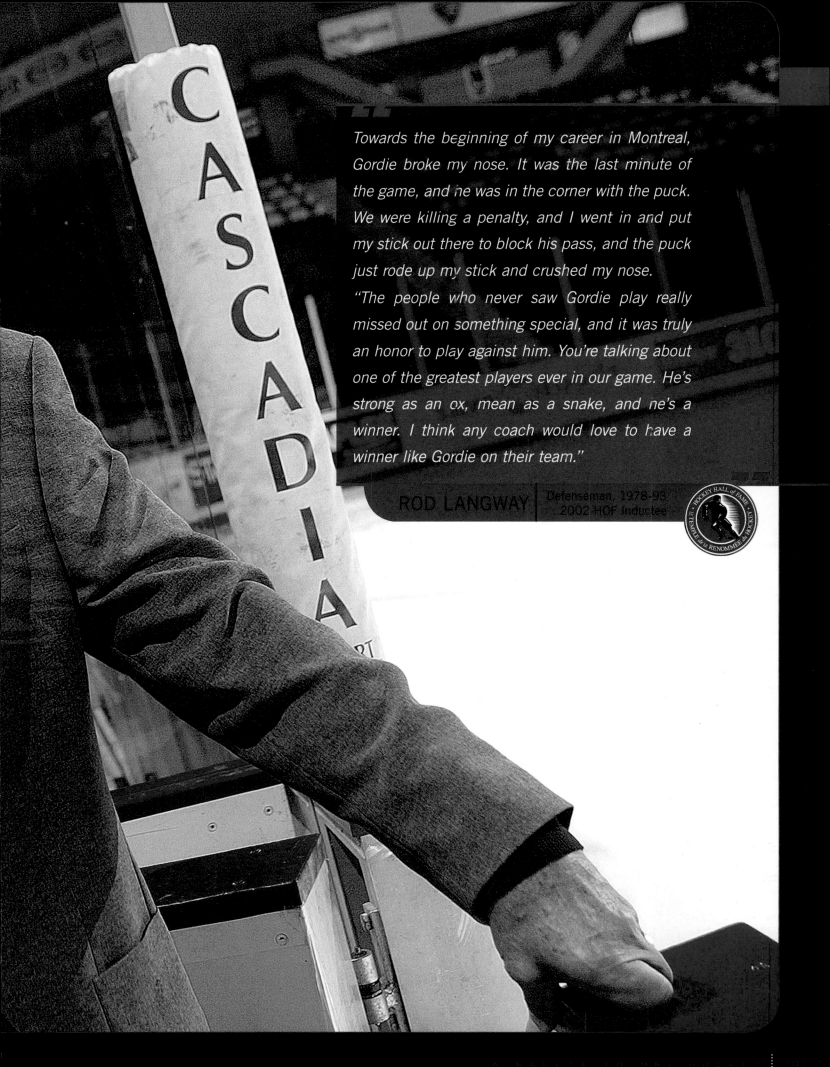

Towards the beginning of my career in Montreal, Gordie broke my nose. It was the last minute of the game, and he was in the corner with the puck. We were killing a penalty, and I went in and put my stick out there to block his pass, and the puck just rode up my stick and crushed my nose.

"The people who never saw Gordie play really missed out on something special, and it was truly an honor to play against him. You're talking about one of the greatest players ever in our game. He's strong as an ox, mean as a snake, and he's a winner. I think any coach would love to have a winner like Gordie on their team."

ROD LANGWAY | Defenseman, 1978-93
2002 HOF Inductee

NINE

Hockey's First Family

No family has given more to the sport than the Howes

There's a melancholy combination in Gordie Howe's voice as he talks about his wife Colleen. Joy and delight mingle with sadness and pain.

because her sense of humor is still strong," Howe explained. "I was helping her get ready for bed and she starting pinching at me and fighting me.

"I said to her, 'You used to like it when I took

had nothing else to do," Howe recalled. "I walked in one day, and there was this beautiful blonde bowling with these three elderly gentlemen."

It was Colleen.

Howe grilled the proprietor of the alley to gain details about the woman who'd made him swoon, finding out she was a regular there, bowling with her grandfather. The shy Howe desperately wanted to meet her, but the most feared skater in the NHL couldn't muster up the gumption to approach the woman who would ultimately become his wife.

"I was kind of like a stalker there for awhile, showing up to bowl, watching her, but never talking to her," Howe said.

Finally, the bowling alley operator introduced the pair. When the two met, Gordie had already won two Hart trophies and three Art Ross trophies, but the ever humble Howe didn't let on about his celebrity. She knew Gordie played hockey, but they dated for a year before Colleen found out the man in her life was the most famous athlete in Detroit.

"I was playing with the New York Rovers, and they called me in and told me that I would be playing against the Red Wings. I think it was a Wednesday night, and I thought, 'Oh, this is going to be a bit of a knee-knocker.' We got out on to the ice to warm-up and they came over and wanted a picture of the two of us. We're standing there and I said, 'I don't know about you, but I'm shaking like a leaf.' He said, 'That's no problem, wait until the whistle blows.' Once the whistle blew, I was all right, but we never were on the ice at the same time in that game.

"The second time I played the Wings was an amazing time because I scored the tying goal in the third period. When the goal went in, Gordie was sitting on the bench and let out a 'Yeah!' "

Vic Howe (Gordie's Brother)
Right wing, 1950-54
New York Rangers

"I was getting ready to go home for the summer to Saskatoon, and we were saying our goodbyes," Howe said. "She wanted me to meet her father." Before Colleen could finish the introduction, her dad, a huge hockey fan, intervened.

"I know who he is," he said.

Colleen grew to not only appreciate what Gordie did for a living; she became the driving force in ensuring he was properly compensated.

As individuals, each being human, the Howes have their strengths and weaknesses. As a team, they're perfect. As husband and wife and as business partners, combining the greatest hockey player of all-time with the most influential woman in the history of the game.

"She did everything for me, and she never let me down," Gordie said.

Together, they raised four children -- sons Mark, Marty and Murray, and daughter Cathy, although at one point, the Wings seemed confused as to how many daughters he had.

Mark and Marty Howe still taunt younger brother Murray with memories of "the doll."

``One year, the Red Wings had a Christmas party," Mark Howe said. "They handed out presents to all the kids. Murray opened his up and it was a baby doll."

Seems that someone in the Red Wings' front office had screwed up and inadvertently identified Gordie Howe's youngest son as a girl. "They thought his name was Marie," Mark said. "We've never let Murray forget that doll. Even to this day, I love telling that story."

``I guess that's the price you pay for being the youngest."

Growing up as Gordie Howe's sons might seem glamorous, and, at times, the boys say it was, but for most of their childhood years life was pretty

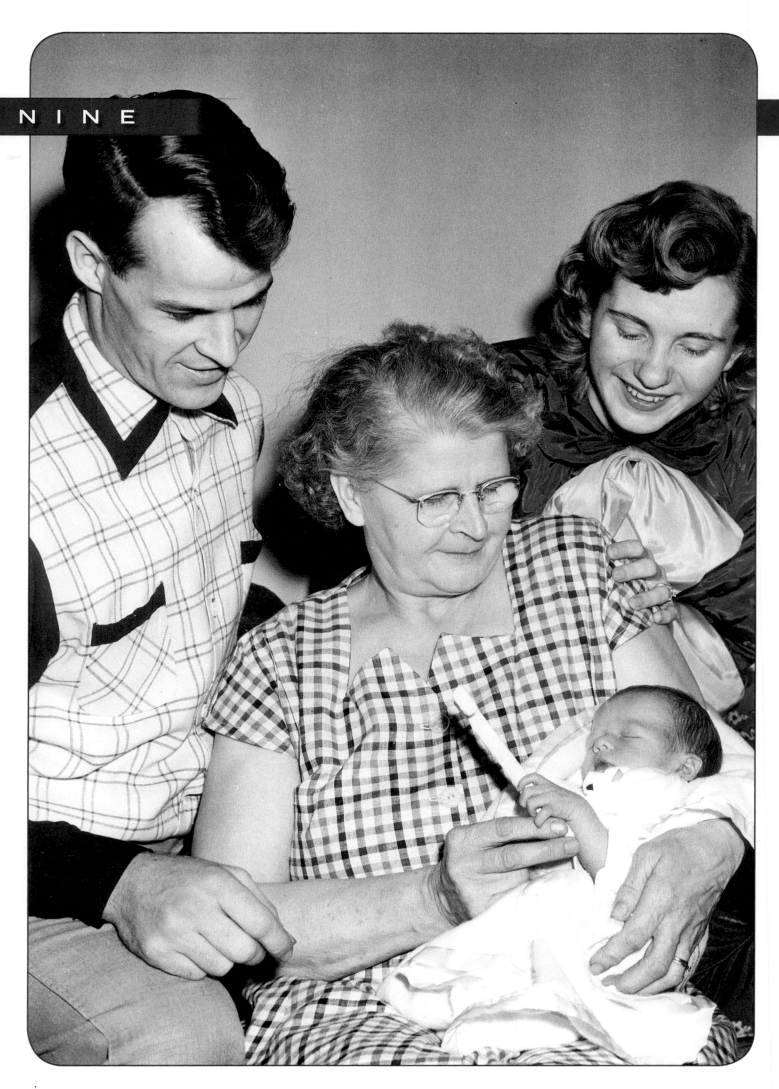

much that of normal brothers.

``Marty and I, we'd beat the crap out of Murray every day,'' Mark said. "Any time the opportunity was there, we took advantage of it. Marty and I, we had our share of fights, too. I think the year (1972) when I went off to play for the (U.S.) Olympic team, and Marty went up to play junior in Toronto -- that really changed us.

``We'd never been separated, all through growing up. We always had played for the same teams. I think, during the time apart, we really missed each other.

``After that, we never really fought again. We'd have the odd disagreement when we were in Houston, but I think the time apart brought us closer together as brothers.''

Despite being Gordie Howe's eldest son, Marty had early designs on becoming a gridiron hero. "I was kind of a greaser in high school," Marty said. "I got to know the principal pretty good. In tenth grade, I was determined to be a football player. I was playing middle linebacker at Southfield Lathrup.

"Mark and I were on a tremendous hockey team that year, but I still had my heart set on football. But there was this one night, I really wanted to play hockey. We were something like 72-1 and were playing the only team that had beaten us. I asked my football coach if I could miss practice, but he told me if I did, I was off the team.

"Well, I went and played hockey and we won. The next day, when I came to football practice, my gear was gone from my locker. So I stayed with hockey and a year later, was off to Toronto to play for the Marlboros."

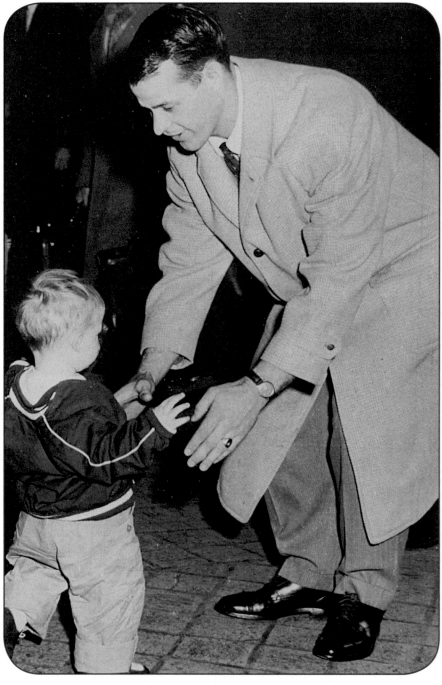

``Marty never really applied himself in school,'' Mark said. "I did well in school, and Murray was probably the one in the family who was the most book-smart."

At first, Murray's goal was to follow his famous father and brothers into the NHL. At five-foot-six, it was going to be a daunting task. Like his brothers, Murray traveled to Toronto to play junior hockey, turning out for the Seneca Nats of the Metro Junior B League.

One of his teammates was Wayne Gretzky, making Murray the only member of the family to play on the same team as the Great One. "My dad always teases me," Murray said. "He says I taught Gretzky everything I knew and then I retired."

The youngest of the Howe brothers tried out for the University of Michigan in 1978, but didn't make the team. "They asked me to come back

the next year, but I just dove into my studies and was pulling straight-As, so I decided to pack in hockey and concentrate on my studies," Murray said. "I had always enjoyed the sciences and it was at that point that I decided medicine was what I was going to try for."

Murray spent a dozen years in Ann Arbor, finishing with four years of residency at the University of Michigan Hospital, where he was one of the team of physicians who helped save the life of Cecilia Cichan, the only survivor of Northwest Airlines flight 255, which crashed after takeoff from Detroit's Metropolitan Airport on Aug. 16, 1987.

Dr. Howe also earned a one-year fellowship to Detroit's Henry Ford Hospital, where he learned how to do magnetic resonance imaging (MRI), a test to determine the seriousness of muscle-damage injuries. The majority of his patients were professional athletes, who were unaware that their doctor was the son of one of Detroit's most famous stars. "I didn't tell anybody, and with my size, not many people would ask me if I was related to Gordie," Murray said. "It was kind of neat, being on the other side of that coin."

Long before he was earning a living by taking pictures of the human anatomy, Murray got a

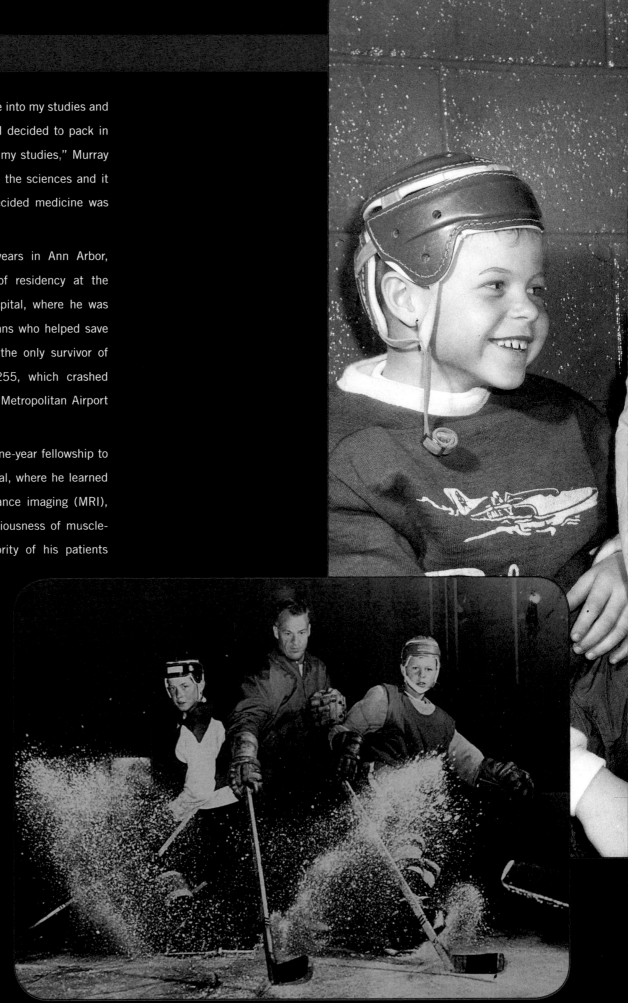

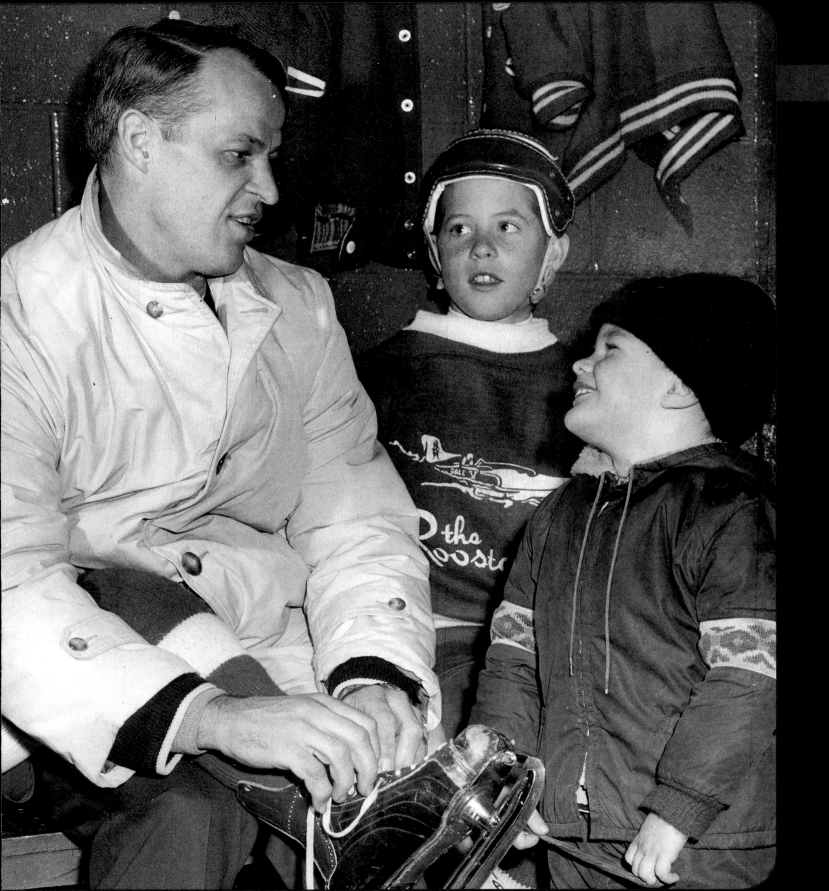

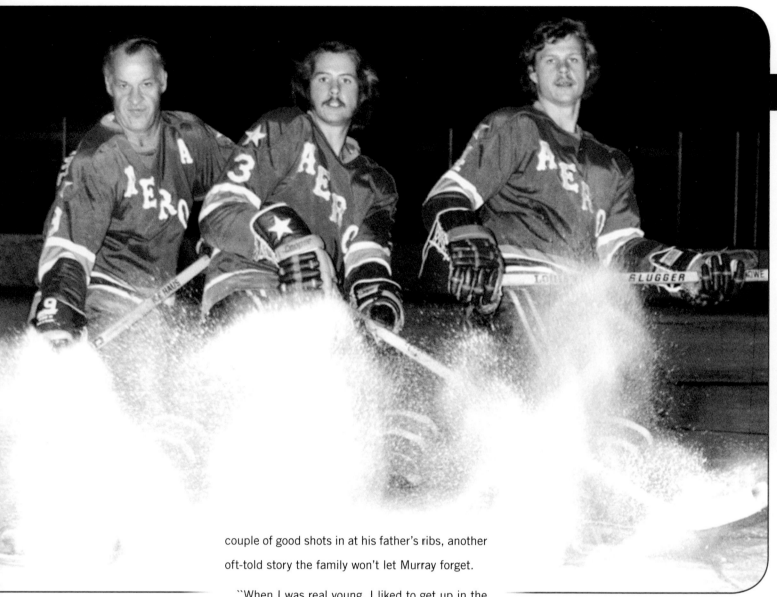

couple of good shots in at his father's ribs, another oft-told story the family won't let Murray forget.

``When I was real young, I liked to get up in the middle of the night and crawl into bed with my parents," Murray said. "My dad had a couple of cracked ribs and had to sleep in a special vest to keep from moving. I was a fidgety sleeper, and I'd thrash around at night. One time, I guess I rolled over and kicked my dad right in the ribs.

``I was too young to remember doing it, but they've never let me forget that one."

``We seemed to have a knack for that," Marty said. "Dad would come through the door after a six-game road trip. The three of us would tackle him and, naturally, hit him right where his latest injury had occurred.

``Overall, dad had it pretty easy, though. We'd be causing trouble and he'd get to leave on a road trip. Mom would have to handle the discipline."

The Howe family factor now goes three generations deep. Today, Mark's son, Travis, handles his grandfather's business affairs.

"Travis is a sharp kid," Gordie said. "He's a lot like Mark, keeps a lot of stuff to himself, but he's very sharp."

For all his unparalleled success on the ice, Gordie's greatest satisfaction comes from his family's achievements. "I don't think anything makes Gordie feel prouder than when one of his kids accomplishes something," Colleen Howe said in a 1995 interview.

"That's quite true," added Gordie. "There's a feeling you get when your kid succeeds." **9**

There are people that are takers, and there are people who are givers. For me, I've always looked at my dad as a kind, gentle person, and he has such a great charisma. He has a certain gift and people respond to him. He's very quiet and doesn't say much. I think a lot of it probably has to do with his upbringing.

"My dad was always taught to keep your eyes open, your ears open, and your mouth shut and you'll learn a lot. But that's how he was born and raised. He was taught to respect everybody and everything. He does have a certain charisma that

"I don't know if it ever dawned on me that my dad was a famous hockey player. To me, he was my dad. People would ask, 'What does he do for work', and I'd say, 'He really doesn't work. He plays hockey.' I didn't think of it as a job, he was just having fun playing hockey, and we would jump on him when we saw him in the morning. We had a great way of finding the sore spot in the morning when we jumped on him. It never failed that we would get him right where it hurt.

"We've always been a close family. Gordie wasn't making much money. He worked in the summer too, so my mom would make our clothes; we grew-up on casseroles. But we were always together and we always ate together when we could. The only time when any of us really split-up was when I went to Toronto to play juniors.

MARTY HOWE | Gordie's Son

NINE

the Comeback

Howe returned to the ice to play with his sons, comes back to the NHL at the age of 51 and to a tumultuous ovation at Joe Louis Arena during the NHL All-Star Game

Howe's long-established personal goal was to play 20 NHL seasons. He far exceeded that expectation, skating 25 campaigns in a Red Wings' sweater.

The 1970-71 season was Howe's last – and perhaps most difficult -- with the Red Wings. New coach Ned Harkness briefly experimented with Howe as a defenseman. Broken ribs and an arthritic wrist cost him 15 games, the most he'd missed since 1947-48, his second season in the NHL.

"I didn't enjoy myself at all the last year," Howe said. "My wrist was so sore I couldn't stickhandle. Management was talking about changes, and it didn't take me long to figure out who they were thinking of changing."

Howe announced his retirement from the game on Sept. 8, 1971, accepting a position in the Wings front office, a move that many assumed was the end of hockey's most storied and productive career.

How wrong everyone would prove to be.

It turned out that as vice president in Detroit, Howe was nothing more than a figurehead. "They gave me the mushroom treatment," Howe said. "They put me in a dark room and threw manure on me."

He sought more input into decisions and when it wasn't forthcoming, Howe jumped at another opportunity to make hockey history. In 1972, the WHA was formed as a rival major league to the NHL. A year into its existence, the Houston Aeros approached Howe with an offer.

How would he like to come out of retirement, join the Aeros and play alongside his sons Mark

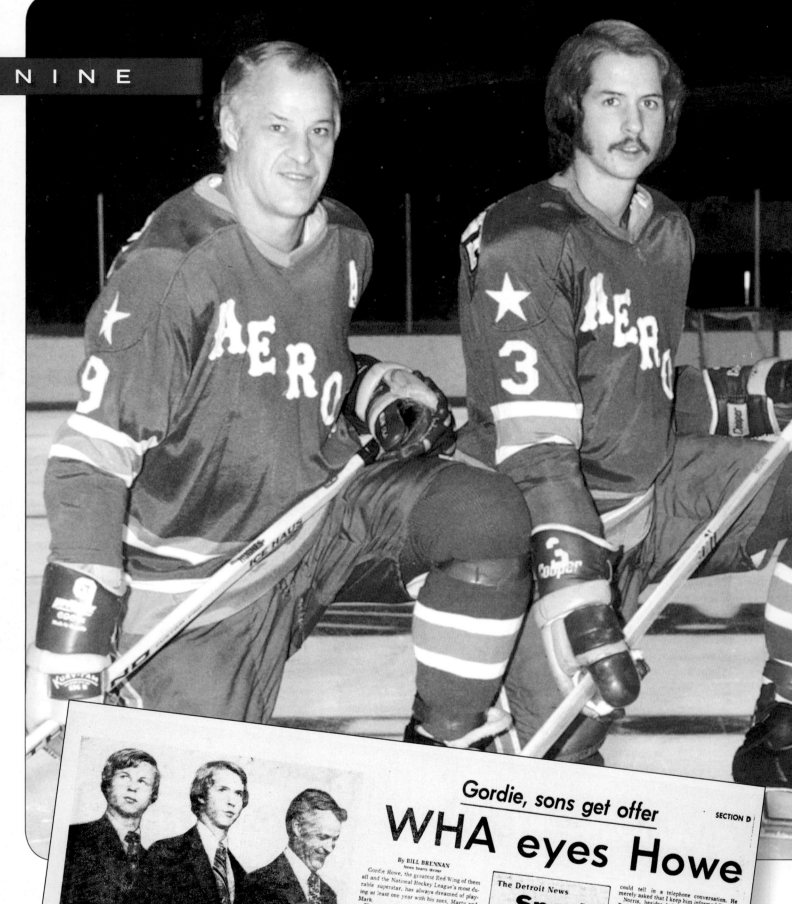

The Howes — Mark (left), Marty and Gordie — are weighing a move to Houston
—UPI Photo

Gordie, sons get offer
WHA eyes Howe

SECTION D

By BILL BRENNAN
News Sports Writer

Gordie Howe, the greatest Red Wing of them all and the National Hockey League's most durable superstar, has always dreamed of playing at least one year with his sons, Marty and Mark.

That dream might come true next season, but if the Howes do play together professionally, it will be for the Houston Aeros of the fledgling World Hockey Association, the NHL's upstart rival.

If Howe plays for the Aeros next season it would be the greatest body blow ever suffered by the Wings. For the NHL, such an action by Howe would be devastating.

"I've talked to them (Houston) and hell, yes, I'm interested," the 45-year-old Howe, who retired as a player a year ago last September, said last night. "Houston wants Marty and Mark and myself and we're going down there, probably later this week to talk about it."

Howe, who is a vice-president in charge of public relations for the Detroit Hockey Club, said he telephoned Bruce Norris, owner of the Wings, last night and told him he was considering the Houston offer.

What was Norris' reaction?

"He asked me to keep him informed," Howe said.

"But for his reaction . . . looking at him to te . . .

The Detroit News
Sports

Bob Sieger, Sports Editor
WEDNESDAY, MAY 30, 1973
Races—6D

could tell in a telephone conversation. He merely asked that I keep him informed."

Norris, besides being owner of the troubled Red Wings, is also chairman of the NHL Board of Governors.

"The main thing with Houston is the boys," said Howe, referring to Marty, 19, and Mark, 18, both stars last season with the Toronto Marlboros of the Ontario Major Junior Hockey League.

"As you are probably aware, Houston drafted both Marty and Mark last month . . . at the same time they apparently put me on the negotiation list.

"It was while we were talking to Houston about the boys that they asked if I would be interested in playing one season with them. They knew my greatest wish has always been to play pro hockey with my sons and when they asked, 'Would you be interested?' I said, 'Hell, yes.'"

HOWE THEN revealed that he is somewhat less than happy in his present . . .

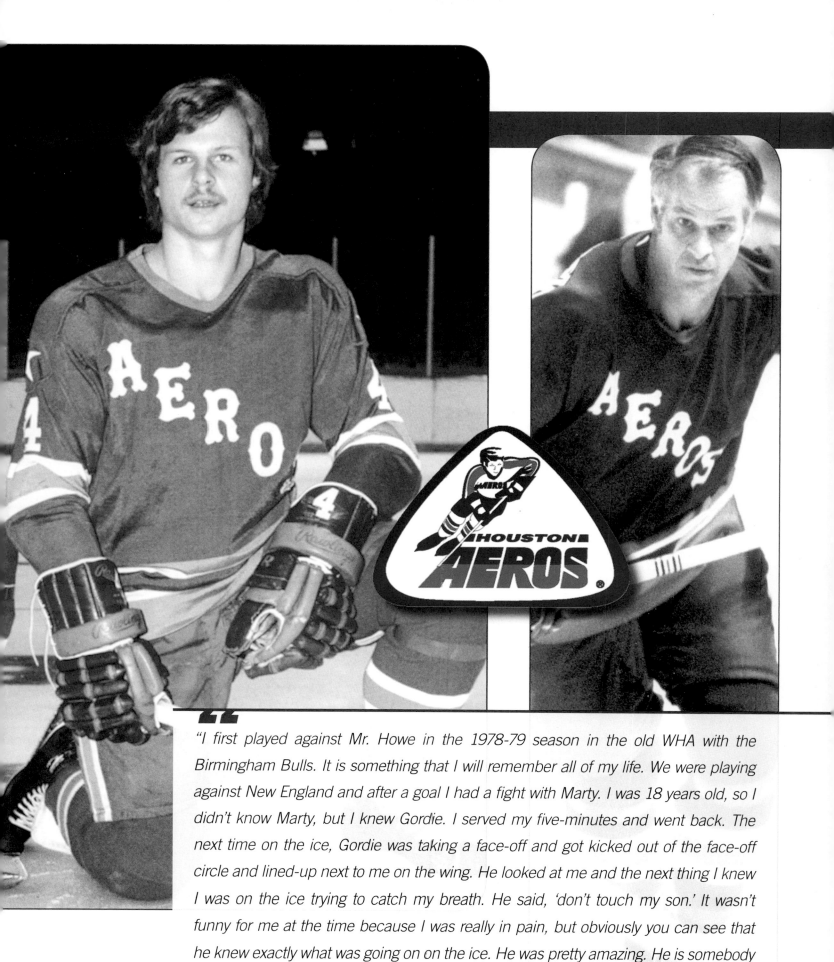

"I first played against Mr. Howe in the 1978-79 season in the old WHA with the Birmingham Bulls. It is something that I will remember all of my life. We were playing against New England and after a goal I had a fight with Marty. I was 18 years old, so I didn't know Marty, but I knew Gordie. I served my five-minutes and went back. The next time on the ice, Gordie was taking a face-off and got kicked out of the face-off circle and lined-up next to me on the wing. He looked at me and the next thing I knew I was on the ice trying to catch my breath. He said, 'don't touch my son.' It wasn't funny for me at the time because I was really in pain, but obviously you can see that he knew exactly what was going on on the ice. He was pretty amazing. He is somebody that we will be talking about for the rest of our lives -- for centuries to come."

MICHEL GOULET | Left wing, 1979-94
1998 HOF Inductee

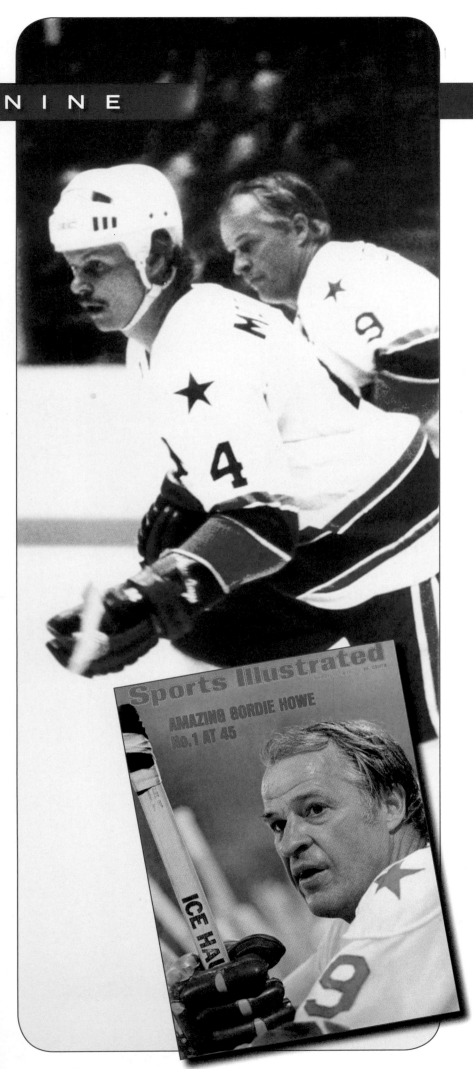

Sports Illustrated

AMAZING GORDIE HOWE
No. 1 AT 45

ICE HA

and Marty, who'd recently signed with the team?

It didn't take long for him to make up his mind. "I made that decision for the love of the game -- to come back with Mark and Marty," Howe said, though the sons were unsure if their dad at 45-years-old, was making the right decision.

"Our first exhibition game was in Greensboro (N.C.) against the Los Angeles Sharks," Marty Howe said. "Gordie was in the starting lineup, and as the puck dropped, the winger opposite him drops his gloves and says, 'OK Howe, lets go.' Gordie just took his stick and hit the guy in the head. They both got majors.

"They come out of the penalty box, and the guy drops his gloves again and says, 'OK, Howe, lets see what you got,' so Gordie cuts him up again. This time, they got majors and misconducts. By the time they're out of the box again, it's nearly the end of the second period, but this guy hasn't had enough yet.

"Well, Gordie could see this guy wasn't going to give up, so he just took his stick, wound-up and cracked the guy right across the head. They both got tossed."

Howe was MVP of the league in 1973-74, and that fall, he got the chance to take on the Russian national team in an eight-game series. The Soviets quickly learned what North American players knew as gospel -- don't mess with the big guy.

"I remember a Russian player slashed Mark in the ear and cut him open," Howe said. "The next shift when we were out together, I had the puck, and he was coming for me. I said, 'Oh, you want the puck? Well, here it is.' I threw it in the corner and when he went to get it, I broke his arm.

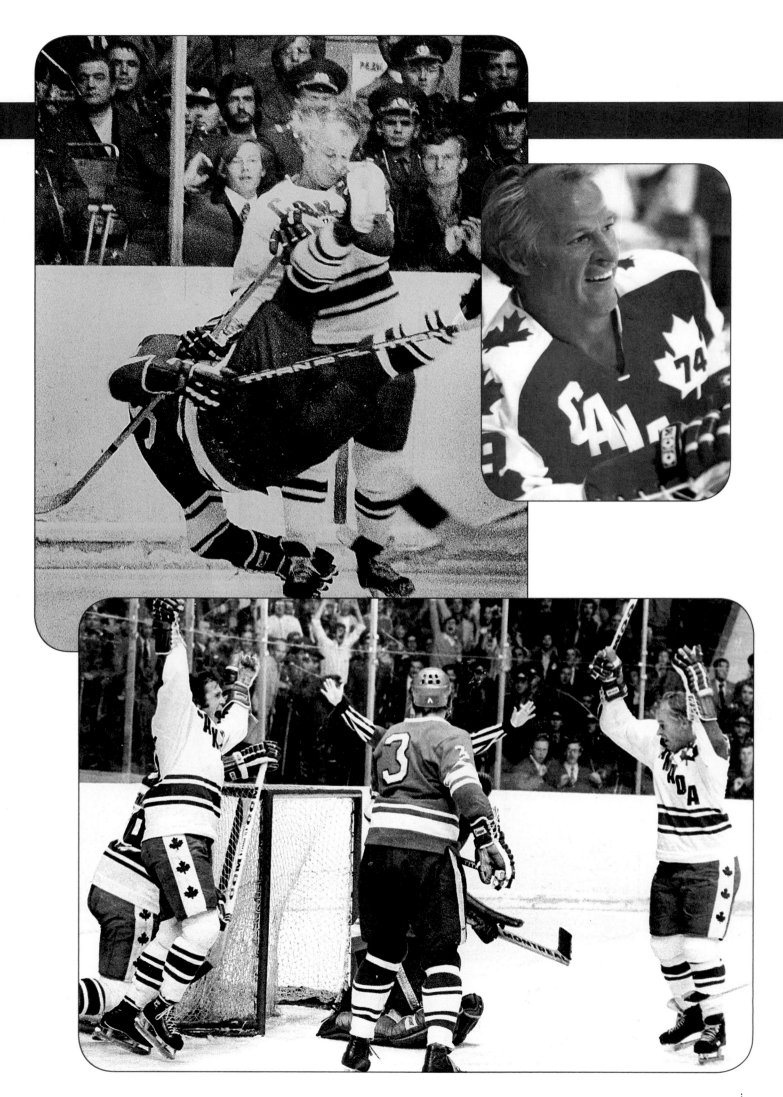

"After the game, he had to shake hands like this," Howe said, reaching across his body and extended his left hand, still smiling devilishly at the memory of the Russian's misfortune.

Another Howe recollection involved his first time playing alongside Wayne Gretzky. It was 1979 with the WHA all-stars against Moscow Dynamo.

"There was a Russian hacking away at Wayne all night, and he was getting really frustrated," Howe said. "I told him, 'The next time you get the puck, bring it up right wing. When you hear heavy breathing, get out of the way.' "

Howe leveled the Russian with a devastating check. As the Russian trainer tended to his prone player, the WHA team changed lines. "We were sitting on the bench, and I said, 'Damn,' " Howe remembered. "Wayne asked, 'What's wrong, Gord?'

"I said, 'He's getting up.' "

The Great One's memories of his first time facing Howe are equally painful. "My second game with Indianapolis in the WHA was against (Howe)," Gretzky said. "I saw Gordie during the warm-up, and he was smiling and winking at me.

"When the game started, we were both on the ice. Gordie had the puck, but I snuck in behind him, stripped the puck off his stick and started heading the

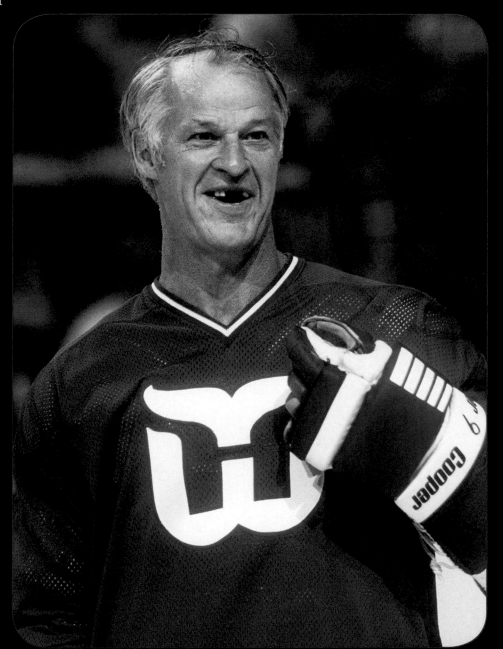

NINE

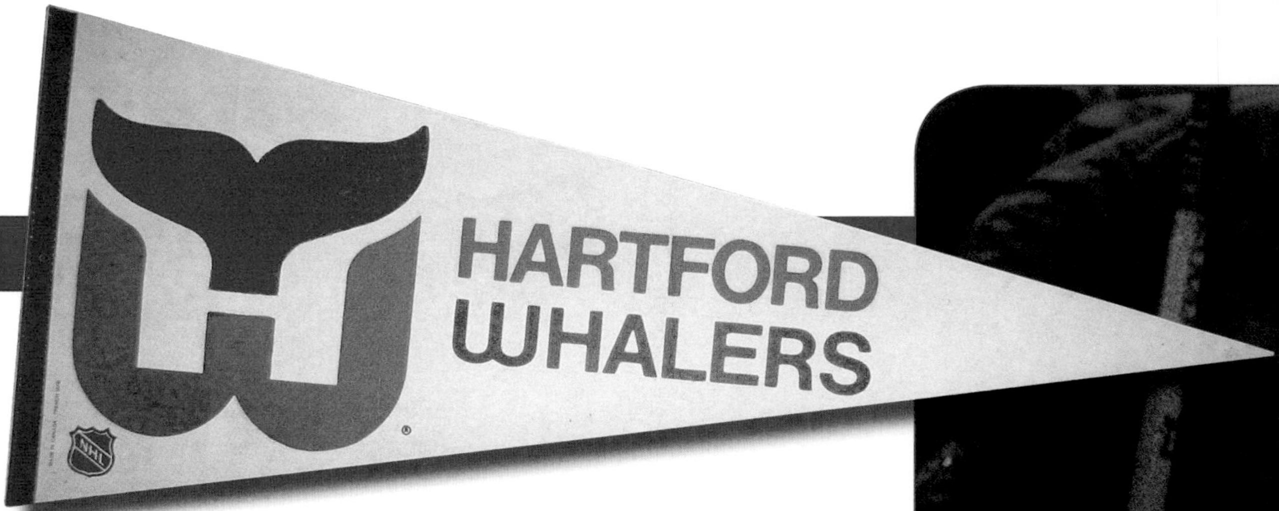

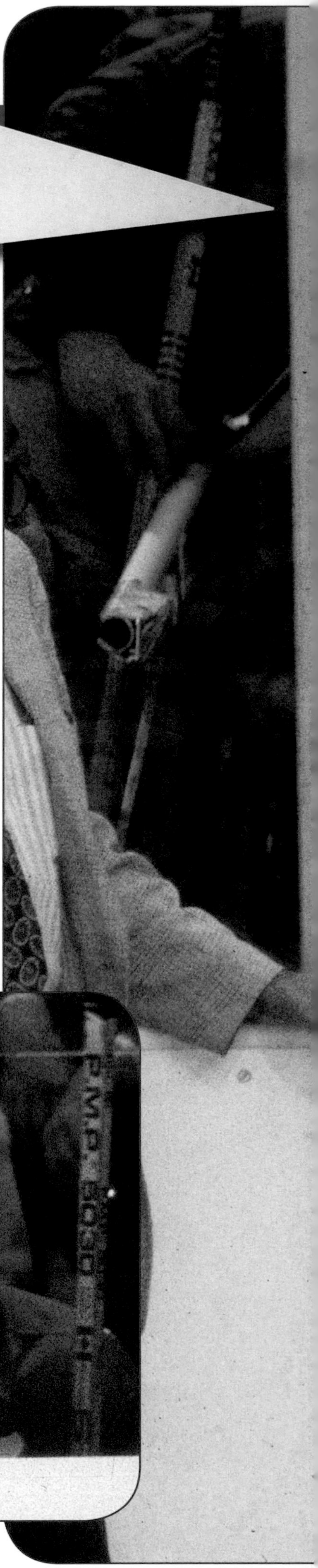

other way. I'd taken about two strides when all of a sudden, I felt this sharp pain in my thumbs. Gordie had whacked me across the thumbs with one arm, spun me around with the other and took off with the puck.

"After a whistle he skated by and said 'Don't ever embarrass me on the ice again.' " The legend's sons know this Jekyll-Hyde side of their dad succinctly.

"He's absolutely the nicest guy in the world off the ice, but once he put that uniform on, look out," Marty said. "I'm just glad I never had to play against him. Practice was bad enough."

The family moved to Hartford in 1977 and played with the Whalers. In 1979, Hartford was one of four WHA clubs usurped in the NHL-WHA merger.

Howe was coming back to the league for a record 26th season.

He played at Joe Louis Arena three times that season. In his first visit, Howe was selected the first star of the game. In his final visit, Hartford coach Don Blackburn put Howe out to start the game at center between Mark and Marty, but it was the middle trip that remains most memorable.

Playing in the NHL All-Star Game, Howe was moved to tears as he was welcomed back to Detroit with a four-minute standing ovation. "It meant everything to me, to be back in the hometown," Howe said.

He retired for a second time in 1980 at age 52 and once the Ilitch family purchased the Wings in 1982, the relationship between the Wings and the

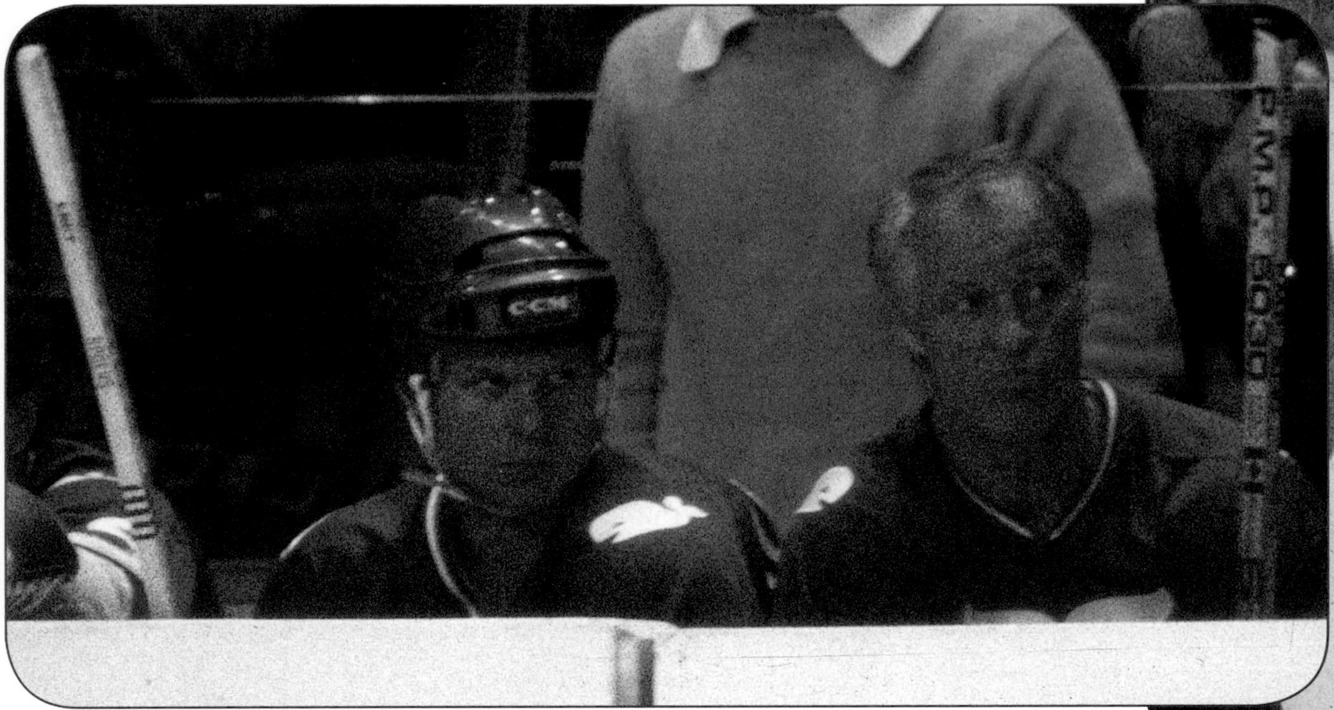

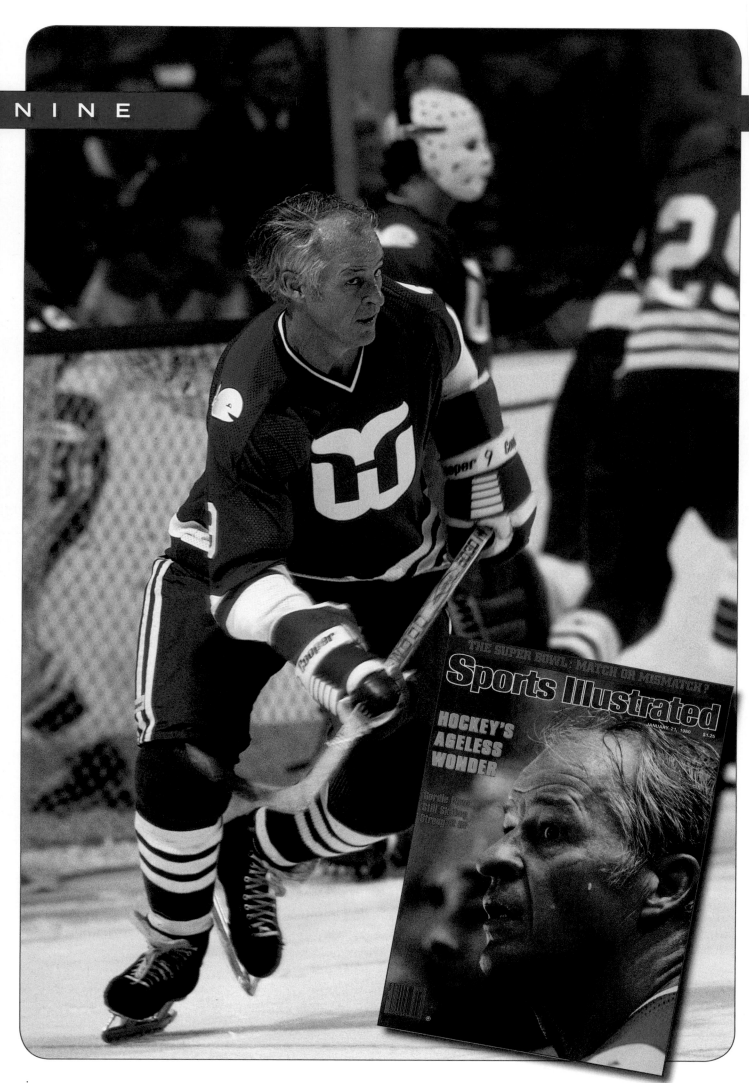

THE SUPER BOWL: MATCH OR MISMATCH?

Sports Illustrated

JANUARY 21, 1980 $1.25

HOCKEY'S
AGELESS
WONDER

Gordie Howe,
Still Skating
Strong at 51

Howes was reborn. Howe's No. 9, retired in 1972, was appropriately hung in the JLA rafters during a 1984 ceremony. He was feted at the rink again on March 31, 1993 in celebration of Howe's 65th birthday. Things had come full circle by the 2006-07 season, when Howe was honored in perpetuity. The JLA West Entance was renamed the Gordie Howe Entrance, and a statue of him commissioned by the Wings and designed by renowned artist Omri Amrany was erected on the spot.

Thirty-three years after the previous ownership essentially shoved Howe out the door, the Wings named one after him. "I like the entrance better," Howe said. "My exit wasn't on a high note."

"Gordie Howe set a standard of greatness with his play that I've always tried to uphold as the owner of this storied franchise," Wings owner Mike Ilitch said. "Gordie was the greatest player of his era and his grittiness on the ice embodied the hard-working spirit of Detroiters. I felt it was important to honor all that he has meant to this franchise and the city of Detroit."

Howe was suitably touched with emotion. "There has always been a tremendous love affair between me and the fans here," he said. "Over the years, I never forgot Detroit," Howe said. "It's always been No. 1 in the hearts of the Howe family."

Likewise, we're sure. **9**

NINE

In Other Words

"When I entered the league, Gordie was toward the end of his career for the first time. But he was still a great hockey player. He had to have wrist surgery and that's the reason, in my firm belief, that he couldn't shoot the puck like he wanted to. He could still skate and all of that, but I noticed that his shot wasn't the same as usual. It got weaker; it seemed, in that last year.

"But even in his 50s he was a force and could still play. He wasn't just there because he was Gordie Howe. He was contributing. I remember he scored a goal on me – a wrist shot from about 25-feet out. He beat me clean to the low catching side. He really got a lot on it – blew it by me before I could get there. I think that's why he came back. He knew he could skate and do the job physically."

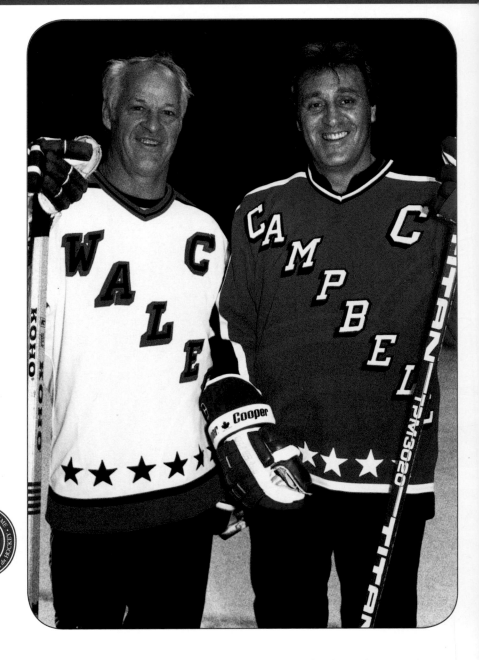

TONY ESPOSITO
Goalie, 1968-84
1988 HOF Inductee

"It was my second game in the NHL and we were playing in the Olympia. I was sitting on the bench and Billy Reay, who was the coach of the Blackhawks said, 'Esposito, you go out there with (Bobby) Hull and let Hull take the face-off.' This is almost the third period. I'm out there and I'm scared. I'm looking around. There's Bobby Hull, Alex Delvecchio, Bill Gadsby, Terry Sawchuk, Glenn Hall, Pierre Pilote, Ted Lindsay, and there's Buck Gordie. I can't believe it. I'm standing on the left wing next to Gordie, and Hull says to me, 'You got that old son-of-a-bitch?' Gordie just looks at me and smiles. The puck drops and I go in to get it and suddenly, wham! He gives me an elbow right beneath the nose in the upper lip. I still have the scare where I got six stitches."

PHIL ESPOSITO
Center, 1963-81
1984 HOF Inductee

"There was one player Gordie was not sure how to take — this was after I was finished and involved with the Bruins. That was Derek Sanderson, he wasn't sure how to take him because he didn't know whether Sanderson was going to hit him over the head, or spear him, or punch his eyes out. But Howe was the ultimate in physical play in the league at that time."

TOM JOHNSON
Defenseman, 1947-65
1970 HOF Inductee

"I met Gordie Howe at the 1981 All-Star Game in Washington. I came down the elevator at the hotel with my mom and dad, and Gordie was standing right there in the lobby and my mother almost fainted. He was always her favorite. I went up and politely introduced myself, and Gordie, being only how Gordie can be – very cordial – said, 'sure I know who you are.' I asked if I could introduce him to my mother, and I'm sure she still remembers that as well.

"Everybody knows the Gordie Howe name and what he has stood for and continues to stand for in the community and in the game. For me, getting a chance to see him was very special. There are only a few guys who can really carry the torch and be true ambassadors in their sport. Gordie is definitely one of them. Of course Wayne (Gretzky) is the other one, but who did Wayne learn from? Gordie."

PAUL COFFEY
Defenseman, 1980-2001
2004 HOF Inductee

"I had the opportunity as a teen -- when I was 13-years-old -- to go to his hockey school at his rink in Saint Clair Shores. I had the opportunity to meet him there and take a picture with him, which I had him sign a couple years ago. I didn't know how it was going to be (at the school), and I didn't want to disappoint him. I had big goals. Just to have the opportunity was a big thrill for me, especially as a 13-year-old coming from northern Ontario into the States. It was a lot of fun. Those memories are still embedded in my mind, when you have the opportunity at a young age to meet a great player like Gordie. It stays with you for a long, long time."

BILL BARBER
Left winger, 1972-84
1990 HOF Inductee

"Playing with Gordie attributed a heck of a lot to my career. He was always very helpful, coming up with pointers and what you're doing, maybe a little bit wrong. He was always helpful and that's always critical. He had everything, so I guess you would say he was sharing it with the rest of us to try and make us better.

"I can recall the guys telling me, 'Hey, get the puck to the big guy and he'll deliver the mail.' He was my favorite target on the right wing. I always tried to set him up the best I could, because I knew he was going to get a goal or get us an opportunity to get us a goal."

ALEX DELVECCHIO
Center, 1950-74
1977 HOF Inductee

"Do I remember playing against Gordie? I sure as hell do. His skill was toughest part of him. He was just a little faster than the rest of us and he could do everything just a little bit better. He was clean. You never had to worry about Gordie taking any cheap shots. As far as I'm concerned, he was one of the best hockey players I ever played against. Gordie played the game hard and he played it well. He didn't play it dirty, but you had to be on your toes to play against Gordie.

"I think Gordie is really right up there in the first 10 (players of all-time). It's pretty hard to put anybody ahead of anybody. At the top, they're all at their best."

CLINT SMITH
Center, 1936-47
1991 HOF Inductee

"There's no doubt that he's Mr. Hockey, the best player in history. I'd have to put Gordie down as the most dangerous opponent I ever faced."

JOHNNY BOWER
Goalie, 1945-70
1976 HOF Inductee

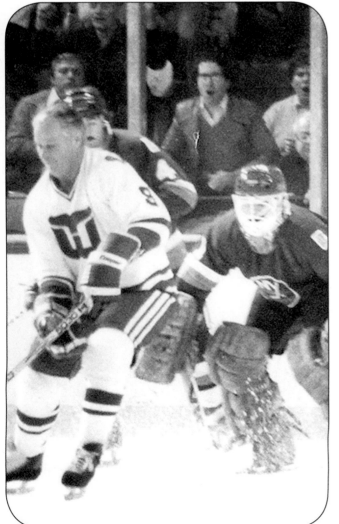

"We were playing in Hartford and I remember facing off against Gordie. It took everything in me not to look up at his head and focus on the jersey, much like when I played my first game in the NHL or the first game in the Montreal Forum. You just don't want to think that you're actually playing against Henri Richard and Gordie Howe and some of those guys. I really felt that I didn't want to be influenced by it, but something happened in the first period that I'll never forget.

"Gordie came in on goal and he shot the puck, of course he was a right-handed shot. The rebound came out and he then switched hands and then shot the rebound at our goalie left-handed. When we got back to the dressing room, I remember Billy Smith saying, 'did you see what he did in the first period?' I said, 'yeah, I saw that. He picked up the rebound with the left hand; he's a right-handed shooter.' And Smitty said, 'I had no idea that he was amphibious.' I love that story and I love telling it when Billy is around."

DENIS POTVIN
Defenseman, 1973-88
1991 HOF Inductee

"I remember playing against Detroit in my second game in the NHL. Johnny Bower got hurt, and I had to play in Toronto against Chicago and Bobby Hull et cetera on a Saturday, and then in Detroit on that Sunday. I'll never forget that game; I was in awe certainly. I call that period BM – 'Before the Mask' -- so you were a little more nervous. Gordie took a shot in that game and snapped my goal stick in half. It had never happened in Juniors, but here was the world's greatest player and he snapped a shot that broke my stick."

GERRY CHEEVERS
Goalie, 1961-80
1985 HOF Inductee

"I met him as a youngster growing up in Oshawa, Ontario. It was an era with Gordie Howe and Bobby Hull, and of course Bobby Orr was coming in. But Gordie was always the man. Everybody loved the Leafs, but once you got outside of that, Gordie was the best in the game. When I look at Gordie I see why he could play until he was 50 years old. He was built to play the game. I always tell people that I was almost too young to remember him, but when I met him he just had a presence. When I talk to guys who played against him, that was his game – he just had a presence out there. He had that presence off the ice as well."

DALE HAWERCHUK
Center, 1981-97
2001 HOF Inductee

"He was usually the best player on the ice every time you played against them. He was very, very strong and you tried to keep him to the outside and hope that he would shoot from a bad angle.

"The one game that I remember happened in New York when Gordie scored his 300th goal, and Andy Bathgate scored for us on a penalty shot and we made the playoffs. But the big thing was Gordie getting No. 300. He was a high producer every year. He'll always be remembered because he played so long and so well, and if I were starting a team, the first two guys I would want are Gordie Howe and Bobby Orr."

HARRY HOWELL
Defenseman, 1951-76
1979 HOF Inductee

I was fortunate that when I started in the league in 1970, I got a chance to play in the old Olympia, and Gordie was playing for the Wings. That was pretty special. Obviously, as a kid growing up, following the National Hockey League, Gordie Howe was the one of the greatest players in my time. So to play against him, I kind of was in awe of him.

"The thing that grew on me was how long he played. We all know Hall of Fame guys that have had successful careers. Some guys played 20 years, I played 15, but 20 is pretty well stretching it. Gordie — he played until he was 52 years old! I kept myself in good shape, even after I retired. And I can still remember when I turned 52, and thinking, 'holy geez, Gordie Howe was still playing pro hockey at that point in time.' To know what your body has to go through each and every season and to play as long as he did was unbelievable."

DARRYL SITTLER
Center, 1970-85
1989 HOF Inductee

So, who's the greatest hockey player of them all?

My first game, Gordie wanted to let the young kid know that he was still around. I made a pass and skated around the net and watched my pretty pass and he knocked me down. I can't say I was surprised. I was just sitting there watching my pass. I had my head down and he drilled me. Surprised? No. I didn't see him coming and it was a good lesson for me in this league. Later on, I had asked him about the hit, and in typical Gordie-fashion said, 'It's better to give than to receive.'

"I've never met anyone like him; in my mind he's the best ever. Nobody will ever touch him. There have been a lot of great players in the past, and they'll be a lot of great players in the future, but none will be as good as Gordie Howe.

BOBBY ORR | Defenseman, 1966-79
1979 HOF Inductee

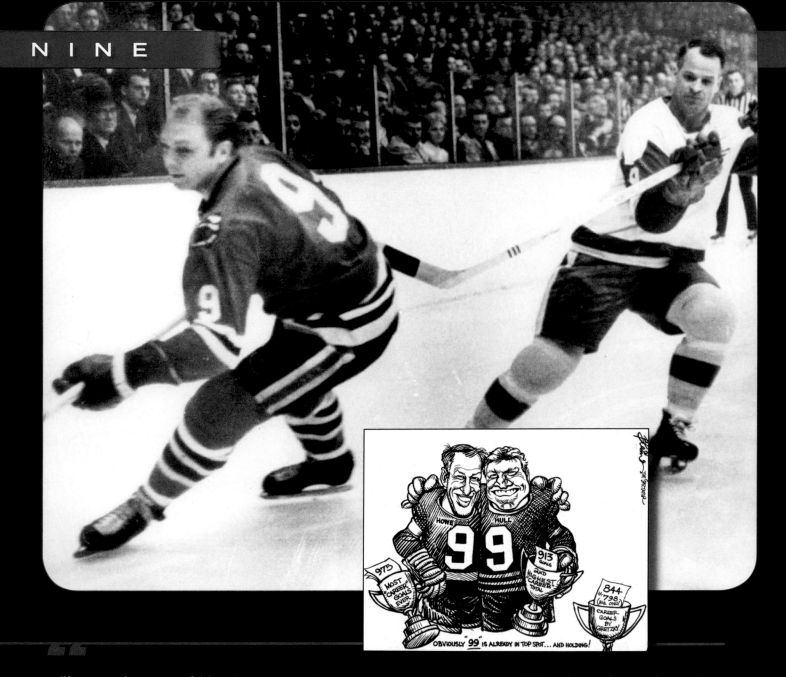

"I remember one of his nights of retiring, when the Vice President (Spiro Agnew) was there. In between the first and second periods Tommy Ivan came in and said, 'Bobby here is a memento that we would like you to give to Howe from the Blackhawks.' I asked if I had to speak and he said no. My three front teeth were in my shirt pocket and a piece of Wrigley's Spearmint was in my mouth. When Mr. Lynch called me up to make the presentation, he handed me the microphone. The crowd was politely applauding. At that time, we had played about 15 years against one another and all that came out of my mouth was 'I've played against this guy and with him somewhat, and I've enjoyed every high-sticking moment of it.' That kind of broke everybody up."

BOBBY HULL | Left wing, 1957-80
1983 HOF Inductee

"In my first four or five years in the league under coach Dick Irvin, we felt that we played Detroit wrong, because our coach wanted to count the hits. A hit was putting the player, the opposition to the ice. And Detroit used to laugh at us because they had a hell of a power play with Red Kelly and Gordie, and Lindsay and Abel. They were in command, and we got beat only by getting stupid penalties.

"Gordie had those big elbows, therefore, you had to be careful when you went around him. You knew you were going to get the stick or the elbow. He caught me a few times. But Gordie never chased and looked for it. He was a natural superstar, like Jean Beliveau. They played hockey, but when they had to play rough, Gordie could do it."

DICKIE MOORE
Right wing, 1951-68
1974 HOF Inductee

"When you're playing against the best player in the league, you're very, very quiet on the ice. That was sort of an unwritten law that, if you know anything about playing, you don't talk to your opponent, especially a high-caliber guy like Gordie. A little talk would get you in trouble, pretty serious stuff, because we often played back-to-back so many times. And (Gordie) had a long memory.

"I always wanted to play with Gordie because we're both from Saskatchewan, we're both half-intelligent hockey players, and I always wanted to play with him, but I never had the chance. I knew of him growing up and seeing him play baseball through Saskatoon. He was a good all-around athlete."

BERT OLMSTEAD
Left wing, 1948-62
1985 HOF Inductee

"I definitely had heard his name growing up and had his (Hartford) hockey card, but didn't get to see him play too much. Growing up in Finland we didn't get the chance to go to games or get too much information on the NHL, but we heard of the big names like Gordie Howe, which was a huge name in Finland.

"I don't know how he did it, but you just look at him and see how strong he was in some of the highlights. I think he really took care of himself, like the players do now, but at that time he was ahead of his time when it came to conditioning, which allowed him to play for so long."

JARI KURRI
Right wing, 1980-98
2001 HOF Inductee

"He was a tough son-of-a-gun and you were always very cautious of what you did to him. He was so strong that he would shove you out of the way. I hit him in the head one time and cut him a bit. By the time that game was over he had retaliated with me and put me in the hospital for seven days. He never even got a penalty. But a lot of times the referees never saw him do things. He was extremely clever that way. . . . Your respect for him grew as time went on."

BOB PULFORD
Center, 1956-72
1991 HOF Inductee

"We knew about Gordie Howe and Bobby Hull in Sweden. They were the main guys, but I never really got to see him play before I got to Toronto and he was playing in the WHA with his sons. When I played against him, I didn't want to hurt him, because all of Canada probably would have killed you. Still, he could take care of himself, and I saw him put his elbow out and hit some guys. He was solid and very hard to move away from the net. It was amazing that at 52 he was still playing, but he was because he was so solid and in such good shape."

BORJE SALMING
Defenseman, 1973-90
1996 HOF Inductee

"Needless to say, playing on a line with Gordie was great. It was great for a young player just coming into the league, who was trying to get established. You couldn't ask for a better winger. Just walking into the Detroit locker room was pretty awesome.

"I was right there for the (Lou) Fontinato fight, 10 feet from where it was happening. It was down behind our net and Gordie was fighting for the puck, and (Fontinato) came charging in from the blue line and grabbed Gordie. I guess he figured he'd show that he was tough. He certainly got a shock."

NORM ULLMAN
Center, 1953-77
1982 HOF Inductee

"The one thing about Gordie is he was really an all-around player in the sense that yes, he was offensive and a goal scorer, but he could also look after himself as well. He could mix it up with the best of them.

"To a lot of Canadian kids and even American kids in the Detroit area, he was Mr. Hockey; just the longevity and the way that he played. He wasn't the flashiest player out on the ice, but he was just there consistently, game after game. He could either score goals or beat you up in the corner, one or the other. And it didn't matter to him which way you wanted to play. . . . I wouldn't go in the corner with him."

STEVE SHUTT
Left wing, 1972-85
1993 HOF Inductee

"In his day, he was one of the bigger players in the league. There were other guys that were pretty good size, but not a lot. I don't think the other guys could use their size as good as Gordie could. He got a lot of room for himself. He was a prototype if you're going to make a hockey player – perfect size, great skater, and terrific eye-hand coordination. He had everything that you want in a player. He was as tough as they made them.

"(In St. Louis) we did warn our team to let him play, don't get involved physically with him and get him after us. One of our young defenseman, Bob Plager, he caught Gordie with a pretty good check, but it was not what we were supposed to do. We paid for it later because Gordie was determined to show his strength. Looking back, it wasn't funny at the time."

SCOTTY BOWMAN
Coach, 1967-2002
1991 HOF induction

"I played against him in Toronto for 10 or 12 years, and then a few years when he came back to play in Hartford with Mark and Marty. It was a nice opportunity, and it was a pretty special night when we played in Detroit and the Howes started the game. That was very, very special. That was never done before, and it certainly won't be done again, where a father and two sons play on the same line to start a game.

"I'll remember just how much he enjoyed playing and what great skills he had, even when he was in his late 40s. He still had great skills. He just enjoyed playing hockey."

DAVE KEON
Center, 1959-82
1986 HOF Inductee

"He had the meanest pair of elbows I've ever seen. He hit me right at center ice. I just happened to be going by him there, and he stuck out that big elbow and knocked me flat on my bum. … I was just surprised because there was no reason for it.

"He filled the arenas. No matter where he played, it didn't make any difference — a lot of them came to see Gordie. …You have a star player, or movie star, or whatever it is — that's what attracts people in there, into the show or the rink. And that's what attracted people in, the way he was able to play hockey. He was just a great hockey player and a great attraction to people."

EDGAR LAPRADE
Center, 1945-55
1993 HOF Inductee

"You couldn't help but notice Gordie because he did everything so easily. He was a great athlete and a great person. He had the right temperament, and the right physical structure. He was muscular and always in exceptional condition. Gordie didn't need the fitness training that players have today. Looking back, I was very fortunate to be playing at the same time he was. We had a lot of great competition. It was fair, and we played by the rules."

ELMER LACH
Center, 1940-54
1966 HOF Inductee

"Playing against him was the thrill of a lifetime. We wanted to pressure him, but we didn't want to hit him because we didn't want a stick in the head. We were telling them in the locker room 'We don't want Gordie scoring against us, but remember, if you go after him you're going to get clunked.' He's the master of trickery, who also has the most experience and style of any player in the history of hockey.

"I was so proud of my (jersey) number. When I came on to the team Clark Gilles was No. 9 and there were only a few numbers available. Our trainer told me I could have 19, but that Craig Cameron had it the year before so it might be too big on me. Well, to have a No. 9 in my number was pretty cool. There were lots of great No. 9s, and Gordie was probably the best, so to have that number I was pretty excited."

BRYAN TROTTIER
Center, 1975-94
1997 HOF Inductee

"I remember my first game at the Olympia. I was unconscious for -- I don't know -- a couple of minutes. Two of my teammates picked me up and were sliding me back to the bench, and one of the linesmen came by and he says, 'No. 9.' He put my lights out, and that was my introduction to the Olympia and the Detroit Red Wings. Then a couple of years ago at an All-Star Game, we were having breakfast in the hospitality room and Gordie comes to me and said, 'Rod, did I ever get you?' I said, 'Gordie, who didn't you ever get? You've done everybody."

ROD GILBERT
Right wing, 1960-78
1982 HOF Inductee

"The thing I do remember, is how strong, physically he was. It was unbelievable. Going into the corner with him, you couldn't get the puck away from him. If he tried to go around you, you'd go to push him up the boards and he would stick an arm out, and with one hand still controlling the puck. It was like trying to push a wall; you couldn't push him off the puck. He was phenomenal. I don't think there was a single weakness in his game. He could play any type of game you wanted to play. You want to play physical? He was strong. He was just perfect. That's why he's Mr. Hockey."

GUY LAPOINTE
Defenseman, 1968-84
1993 HOF Inductee

"Stan Mikita has told me that Gordie was tough. That's what you hear the most. He was a great hockey player, but he was tough and gritty. Nobody really messed with him because you knew you were going to get it back. And when you played a team 12 times in a season, at some point you knew, he was coming. They had long memories back then.

"In his day, most of the players had a straight blade stick. Obviously, if they had the equipment that we have today, especially Gordie – the way he was built, his forearms, his shoulders – he would have been a hard, hard shooter. That to me says a lot about those guys; how they played in their day, especially him, as great as he was. It was an even field, but it was probably a lot more difficult to score than it is today."

DENIS SAVARD
Center, 1980-97
2000 HOF Inductee

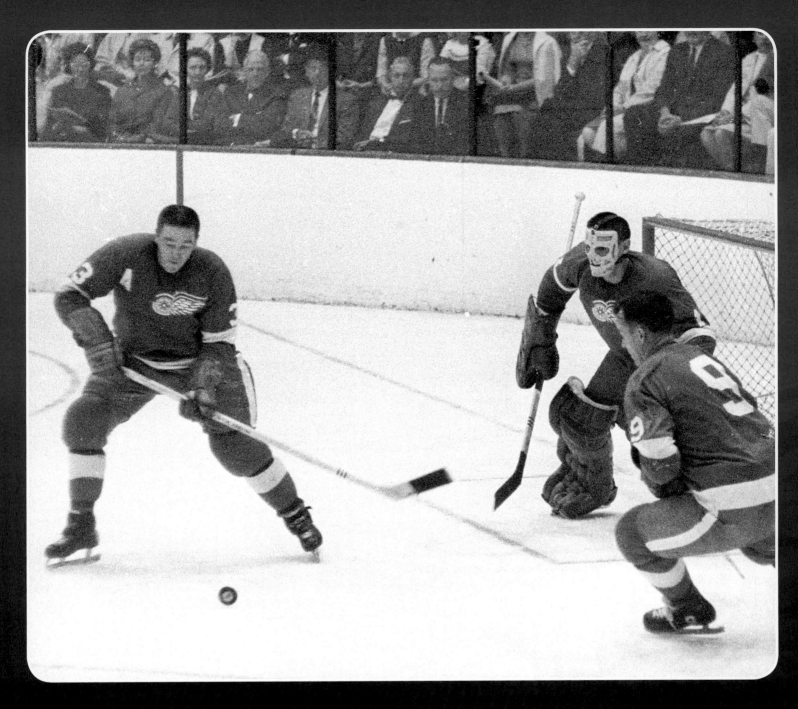

"When we traveled, we would take a bus to the airport. Gordie always waited in the lobby to see if everybody was on the bus because (Jack) Adams wouldn't leave without Gordie. He would say, 'Where in the hell is he?' You'd say, 'I just saw him in the lobby, Jack.' Then Gordie would saunter over and Jack would look at him and not say a single word. Gordie did that so if we had any stragglers they wouldn't have to incur Adams's wrath. He definitely left others behind; he left Howie Young behind a couple of times. Gordie was always the last on the bus because he knew if a guy wasn't there that Adams would leave."

MARCEL PRONOVOST
Defenseman, 1949-70
1978 HOF Inductee

"My mom (Dorothy) was a huge fan of Gordie Howe's from when I was a real young kid. I found out, once I got older, that my mom sent a birthday card to Gordie every year. When I finally did make it into the NHL, and played against Gordie at the Nassau Coliseum for the first time, my mom happened to be in town, and she was able to meet Gordie Howe after the game. It was a huge thrill for her. It was a bigger thrill for me to introduce her to Gordie.

"It was always special playing against Gordie. I remember the first time playing against him in Hartford and it was a little surreal because I had been watching him ever since I was a little boy, watching hockey on TV. It was quite amazing, and as I get older I find it quite amazing that he was able to play until that age."

MIKE BOSSY
Right wing, 1977-87
1991 HOF Inductee

"You have to respect everything that he did. He was a superstar. I didn't play against him, at least that I remember anyway. Everybody knew of Gordie Howe when we were growing up, I mean him, Jean Beliveau, all the superstars. Certainly, in his era, Gordie Howe was the best. In different eras there are different guys. In my era there is Wayne Gretzky and Bobby Orr. I think Bobby Orr was one of the best all-around hockey players, and Gordie Howe was the same thing."

BILLY SMITH
Goalie, 1971-89
1993 HOF Inductee

"It was basically that he was in such good condition in his career. And he used such a short hockey stick and used it to protect the puck, which is something a lot of us didn't realize.

"I was up and down two times with the Rangers before I got to play against Gordie, but Edgar Laprade warned me about No. 9. He was playing center and I was 19 years old then. He told me to be careful of No. 9, because he's good with the elbows and the stick. We called him Mr. Elbows before he was called Mr. Hockey."

ANDY BATHGATE
Right winger, 1952-68, 1970
1978 HOF Inductee

"Gordie looked after me. If anyone gave me a cheap shot, he took care of them. He was my idol. I used to sit on the bench and just watch him. I never took my eyes off of him. I took the compassion that he showed the younger guys and tried to do the same thing as the captain in Boston. I got the idea of looking out for the kids from Gordie.

"I can't say enough good things about him. He's a friend. He had a great career and I'm sure he was proud to play with his two sons. That was something. I'm just proud to call him a close friend."

JOHNNY BUCYK
Left winger, 1955-78
1981 HOF Inductee

"My first experience of meeting Gordie Howe was when my dad worked for Eaton's in Canada. We had an Eaton's department store in Moose Jaw, Saskatchewan. Gordie used to come around and sign autographs. It was some 50 years ago now. At that point, I didn't know exactly who he was and the fact he was an NHL hockey player. Little did I know that he would turn out to be who he was and turn out to be Mr. Hockey of all things.

"I actually played against Gordie and I think my only focus before the game was to skate next to him. I was 24 in those days, and he was what, 52? My only thought process at that point was to skate with him, don't let him touch the puck, and don't make him mad because there's all those stories of him with the elbows and with the stick. And I just said, 'You know what? I'm not here to make enemies; I don't need to hit Gordie Howe to be famous.' So I just skated next to him, and it was a pretty calm evening the few times I did play against him."

CLARK GILLIES
Left winger, 1974-88
2002 HOF Inductee

"The fact that I'm from Saskatchewan, Gordie meant so much to anybody who grew up in Saskatchewan because we all dreamed about playing in the NHL, and he was the king of hockey.

"It was such a great thrill because I actually got to play with him in the All Star Game in Detroit in 1980. It was Wayne Gretzky's first All Star game and Gordie's last. And I got to play in that game. It was one of the biggest thrills I've ever had.

"No one played that long. I was 23 years old, and Gordie had been around forever. To be in the same locker room, to be on the same ice, to be on the same bus over to the game, it was such a thrill. I would have never dreamed of that. From growing up in Saskatchewan where everybody always talks about Gordie Howe — my father, my friends and their dads — he was the greatest hockey player to ever play. Everybody just drooled over that fact that I was getting the chance to be on the same ice with Gordie. So it was quite a thrill for me."

Bernie Federko
Center, 1976-90
2002 HOF Inductee

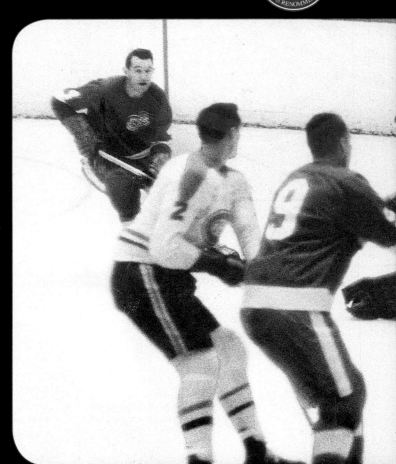

"I respected him very much so, and evidently he must have respected me. He's a big, strong guy, but if you played him without messing around with elbows and everything, he'd do the same to you. But if you kind of did something to him, he'd do the same to you.

"He meant an awful lot to the game. I put him way up top with Gretzky and all the guys that are now playing that you hear so much about. I think that you take guys like him, Milt Schmidt, Teeder Kennedy and Ted Lindsay … they did an awful lot for the game. They were colorful players, they were tough players, who came to play every night. I respect him as one of the greatest hockey players. Not only that, but a real gentleman. Off the ice, on the ice, he always carried himself well. He represented the Wings like nobody else."

FERN FLAMAN
Defenseman, 1944-61
1990 HOF Inductee

"My first NHL game I played against Detroit. I was 19 years old. I was so lucky not to play against Gordie because Gil Tremblay was a left wing and Gordie was a right wing. So I was very happy to play against him, but on the other side. Especially with my height, I think I would have had a problem, but Gil Tremblay's mission was to watch Gordie Howe, since he was a special player. You don't have too many guys like him very often.

"He controlled the game. When he was on the ice, he carried the puck very nicely. In comparison, he was a guy like Bobby Orr. When you were with those guys on the ice, they just controlled the game."

"I was very young, and back then we played a lot against each other. I think the respect was there. Maybe that's why when we see each other now, the respect is very high. For me, you cannot say enough about Gordie. He's really nice with the public, too. It's what hockey needs -- a guy like that to represent the best game in the world."

YVAN COURNOYER
Right winger, 1963-79
1982 HOF Inductee

"When I played junior hockey, my three years in St. Catherines, Ontario, I wore No. 9. Back in the Original Six, there were certain numbers like 9 and 4, they were usually the best players, like the Rocket. Looking back, Gordie was the man. He was everything. I was totally impressed with him, especially looking at pictures of him playing hockey — wow, what an athlete, it's unbelievable.

"I think what impressed me the most was when I first met him. I got drafted by the Red Wings, and then I knew exactly what the man was all about. My dad was a big man at 6-foot-1, 240-pounds, and there you are with Gordie, and everything I had heard about him was right there in front of me. The saddest part for me was he retired the year I turned pro with the Red Wings. I was really looking forward to being with him. But I was so impressed with his demeanor and his closeness to my family, so I had tremendous respect for him."

MARCEL DIONNE
Center, 1971-89
1992 HOF Inductee

"I met Gordie many times. But the first time I met him was when I was 18 and playing in Cincinnati, and Gordie was playing for the (New England) Whalers in the WHA. I'm lining up for the face-off and Gordie is lining-up against me. I'm thinking that I'm on the wrong ice. That season I was fortunate to be selected to play in the '79 WHA All-Star Game in Edmonton. Gordie was there as the Whalers' representative. I asked him "Can I get my picture taken with you?" There we are standing in our WHA All-Star sweaters. It's one of the favorite pictures that I have. He was always a gentleman off the ice and there's always been a genuineness to him.

"He obviously got a tremendous amount of respect, and he could go into the corner and come out with the puck and he still had a great shot. I tried to stay away from him. I remember playing against him in Washington. We had Ben Gustafsson, who hit Gordie. It was an unwritten rule that you don't hit Gordie, and he was upset. The next time they were in the neutral zone, Gordie throws him a flying elbow. Ben saw it coming and ducked, and Gordie wasn't happy."

MIKE GARTNER
Right winger, 1979-98
2001 HOF Inductee

"He was a lot easier to play with than he was against. He was No. 1 — the greatest hockey player I've ever seen. He had a touch around the net. He was strong, and you couldn't move him from in front of the net if he wanted to be there. He was just a great hockey player. He knew the game so well; he knew what was going to happen.

"I remember when I played with him, I used to watch at the other end and he would anticipate the plays so well. He would work his way into a hole and make it easier for Teddy, who was playing with him at the time, and Dutch Reibel or Alex Delvecchio, whoever was at center. He would move into a position to give them a chance to give it to him."

GLENN HALL
Goalie, 1952-71
1975 HOF Inductee

"There is one thing about Gordie that I will always remember: as a defenseman, anytime you went into the corner with him, you had to be careful. If you tried to push him around, or anything like that, the first thing you had on your nose was his elbow. He was very good at that. He was a great competitor, always a team player, and a great asset to the game."

JACQUES LAPERRIERE
Defenseman, 1962-74
1987 HOF Inductee

"There was a fight one time down in Montreal. Gordie and Rocket never played against each other. Usually, they had the checking line against the Richard line and they'd have a checking line against the Howe-Lindsay-Abel line. So they never got on the ice too often against each other. But they did this one night in Montreal. And for some reason or another, they came together in the corner and the elbows got up a little high and the puck came out of there down to the other end. They came again together in the corner, and they dropped their sticks and started to fight. King Clancy was the referee, and all of us players were in a circle. Clancy came in and said quickly, 'Let 'em go! Let 'em go!' He wanted to see who was the best, I guess.

"They both landed a couple blows, and Rocket fell forward, slipped and went down. He was at the feet of all the players who were in the circle around the fight. And he came up and out of that circle and Sid Abel was there, and said, 'What, Rocket? Did you finally meet your match?' Boldly, Rocket broke Sid's nose with a punch. There wasn't a decision there, but it looked like an even match to me. You couldn't say one was better than the other in that fight."

RED KELLY
Defenseman, 1947-67
1969 HOF Inductee

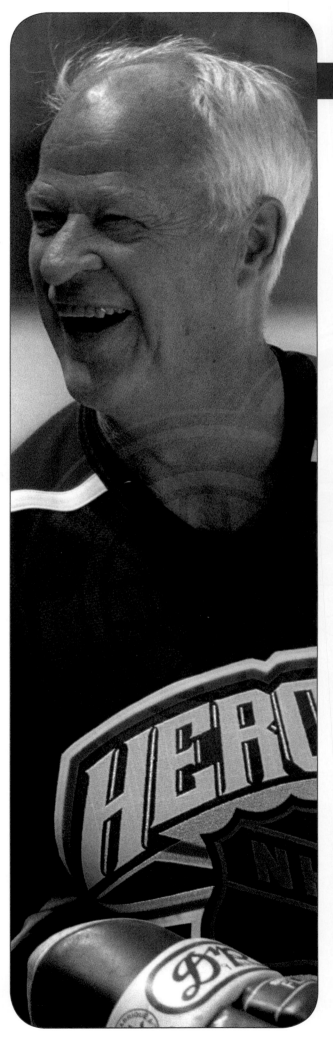

"I first impression when he came back was that he just wanted to play with his sons. But then after playing against him, you were like, 'Holy cripes, he's not just playing with his sons; he can really play!' He has to be one of the most incredible athletes that I've ever met in my lifetime.

"Everyone still talks about Wayne and rightly so, but I still think one of the greatest hockey players to ever play the game is Gordie Howe. You listen to all of the old guys from the Canadiens, and how they talk about Gordie. You can just see what he was for the league and what he's meant for hockey."

LARRY ROBINSON
Defenseman, 1972-92
1995 HOF Inductee

"I had met Gordie Howe at one of the All Star Games. Meeting him at a young age made a huge impression on me. After all, he is Mr. Hockey. Growing up I always heard stories from my dad about how he played the game. He was a physical player with great offensive ability. He played with an edge and always stuck up for his teammates. What can you say about a guy that has a hat trick named after him? If you couldn't get the real thing his was next best."

CAM NEELY
Right winger, 1983-96
2005 HOF Inductee

"The 1980 NHL All-Star game in Detroit is seared in my memory. I remember standing on the blueline during the pre-game introductions, as Gordie Howe stepped onto the ice. Joe Louis Arena exploded. It was a blistering ovation of welcome, of respect, of esteem, of gratitude that seemed would never end.

"He had left an indelible mark on the Red Wings, on the City of Detroit, on hockey. The people there wanted him to know that, wanted him to know how they felt, and told him with an ovation reserved for only the greatest of the greats. I was there, and I will never forget it."

BOB GAINEY
Left winger, 1973-89
1992 HOF Inductee

"My first year, 1965, I was with the Boston Bruins, and Gilles Marotte was a big, tough guy, who hit Gordie along the boards at the old Olympia. When you came out of the one corner at the Olympia there was a door, and Gordie went right through it. Marotte was a big kid, but he was a rookie. And about three shifts later, Marotte had a broken jaw. Somehow the old man got back at him. Gordie was the best, the king of the hill. What else can you say?

"He represents the game so well, and that makes him so special. The way he handles himself in different situations. He's always been a classy person. The only way to describe an individual like this is that he was always one step ahead of the rest. He was blessed with so much."

BERNIE PARENT
Goalie, 1965-79
1984 HOF Inductee

"I was at the Olympics in Lake Placid in 1980, and just before the Games, there was the All-Star Game in Detroit. We were in North America for the show that Gordie Howe put on – I could not believe it. The man was dominating, and the people were going crazy. For us, to watch it on TV, it was a tremendous, emotional experience, that somebody could be that loved and that well respected. There were too many things to fathom, to comprehend. He wasn't average, he was better than average. I never got to play against him, but it was the first time I got to watch him and it was very, very impressive."

PETER STASTNY
Center, 1980-95
1998 HOF Inductee

"When I was a kid, of course, I thought my brother, Maurice, was the best hockey player that I had ever seen. He was my brother. Then, when I grew-up and I saw Gordie, I thought he was one of the greatest too. I know there have been many great hockey players, but those two were the best.

"Sure, I remember the first time I played against Gordie, I got an elbow in the face. He was just a great hockey player, he just wanted to win and that was part of the game. Everybody has his own way to play the game, and he was a little dirty, but just a great hockey player. I hated playing against him because he was too tough."

HENRI RICHARD
Center, 1955-75
1979 HOF Inductee

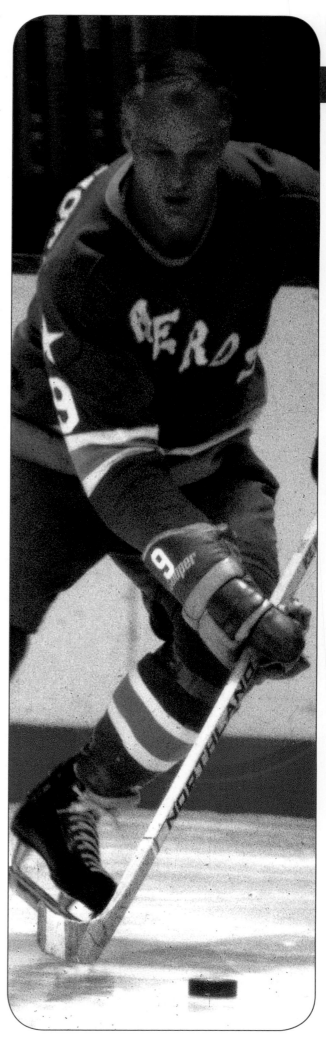

"I didn't have a chance to watch him play too much, but having the chance to meet him on so many occasions, I've been so impressed with the man. Sure, there are the records and the things that he has done on the ice. But my impression of him is more of a personality and the presence that he has.

"We played in a charity hockey game in Boston, and I always wanted to have a picture taken with Gordie. We were in the locker room and he couldn't have been kinder or more generous. He had the picture blown-up and he signed it, 'Good luck with everything you do.' We have a little hockey rink and we put in a locker room for the kids, so I have that picture hanging in the center of it, so you see that picture of Gordie and myself."

PAT LAFONTAINE
Center, 1983-98
2003 HOF Inductee

"I remember going to Le Colisee at the time and I was watching the Houston Aeros' practice. A friend of my mom and dad's -- Gordon Labossiere, who played for the Houston Aeros and the NHL – had us there for a practice, and I remember seeing Gordie at one of the morning skates. I didn't get to meet him; I guess we were all shy. I couldn't speak English at the time, but we were really impressed to see him there.

"I've met him many times at different NHL events. You were always impressed with the way he deals with people. Here's a guy, who was really intense on the ice and even dirty at times, and be so kind and so nice off of the ice. It's such a huge contrast. He has set an example for all of us."

PATRICK ROY
Goalie, 1984-2003
2006 HOF Inductee

"I remember the All-Star Game in Detroit when Scotty Bowman, who was the coach, got every forward to skate on Gordie's line for one period. It was great to play with him for one period. It was a fantastic feeling. Gordie Howe was always looked upon to be Mr. Hockey. He was a real gentleman.

"I remember one game at the old Madison Square Gardens on 49th Street when Gordie lost his hockey stick. He then skated by our bench and he grabbed the first stick that he saw, which was Orland Kurtenbach's stick. He grabbed it and kept playing with it. Kurt jumped on to the ice and chased Gordie trying to get his stick back. It was a real funny thing.

"There's no doubt that Gordie's the most-prolific player of his era. He's just a phenomenal individual to have played as long as he did."

JEAN RATELLE
Center, 1960-81
1985 HOF Inductee

"I was neighbors with Mark Howe. We lived a couple of houses apart in Philly, and my daughter (Jody) went to school with his son (Travis); they were in preschool, about four-years-old. My daughter came home from school one day, and I asked her, 'How did things go in school?' And she said, 'Oh, dad, we had a great time. Travis's grandpa was there and we were playing horsy with him.' They were all riding Gordie's back, and all I could think was there's my idol, Gordie.

"When I played with Mark and we went into Hartford to play, he said that his dad was coming in to see him after the game. I remember sitting in my uniform for a long time, scared to shower in case I missed him, and I had already played against him for a lot of times. I just wanted to shake his hand. . . . For a man of his stature, in any hockey player's eyes, he's very comfortable to be around. You would almost be intimidated, but once you met him, he was such a neat guy."

BOBBY CLARKE
Center, 1969-84
1987 HOF Inductee

"I started watching hockey back in 1952, and Gordie was just coming into his prime. I was in Toronto and when he came to town, he was definitely the guy you wanted to see. He was the star. He was the best all-around forward in the game of hockey. We see players like Gretzky and Lemieux, who are great offensive players, but they weren't great checking players. They didn't have to be. But in Gordie's day, in a six-team league, you had to be a good two-way player."

JIMMY DEVELLANO
Senior Vice President
Detroit Red Wings

"I got to spend a lot of time with Gordie at the (2007) NHL Awards Show in Toronto. We were supposed to fly out that morning along with Gordie, Kenny Holland and Nick Lidstrom. Then the flight was cancelled out of Detroit. It turned into an all-day event sitting at the airport and waiting. Finally, we ended up flying with Chris Ilitch on his jet to Toronto. It was quite the day, we spent the whole day together, which was probably the most time I've had to sit with Gordie. It was cool. It was very interesting. We got there just in time for the show, and there are Gordie and I running off to a dressing room trying to get our tuxedos on for the event."

LARRY MURPHY
Defenseman, 1980-2001
2004 HOF Inductee

"You probably noticed that I eventually wore No. 9. Ronnie Ellis and Gordie Howe were two right-wingers – both who wore No. 9, and my all-time favorite players. In Gordie's final game in Toronto he scored a remarkable goal. He came in over the blue line about 8-12 feet, dropped a shoulder, took a wrist shot for the top corner, and Mike Palmateer, who prided himself on having the best glove-hand in hockey – was still bent over looking for the puck as the light went on. Our entire bench stood up as one and started to cheer. It was wonderful and such a nice way to say good-bye, especially at the Maple Leaf Gardens. It was Gordie Howe. It was vintage, and it was great being a part of it."

LANNY McDONALD
Right wing, 1973-89
1992 HOF Inductee

"He's such a nice man, and I guess that's the biggest impression that's left after you meet him. Anytime you get to meet somebody of Gordie's stature, it's someone that you try to be like. Seeing him deal with people and how he's nice to everybody, that was one of the biggest impressions. He has time for everybody and he's nice to everybody. . . . Life would be a lot simpler if everyone were like Gordie Howe."

GRANT FUHR
Goalie, 1981-2000
2003 HOF Inductee

"When I was a kid, Gordie was one of my idols. I had his book that my dad gave to me for Christmas when I was 12. . . . The first time I played against Gordie, I was so impressed because I had followed his career as a kid. He was one of the top players in the NHL, so for me it was a pleasure of getting the chance to play against him.

"The thing is, some times when I was beside him on the ice, he used to talk to me, and say, 'Hey, you better watch out tonight,' and he would say it laughing. It was actually kind of funny."

GUY LAFLEUR
Right wing, 1971-85, 1988-91
1988 HOF Inductee

"The first time I played against him was in Springfield because the arena in Hartford wasn't ready. I couldn't believe it; I was playing against a legend. It was just incredible. I had always heard of the type of player he was and how he played the game with so many different dimensions to it. You didn't mess with him in his time or that night, which was proven to me at that age. The story I remember about that game is that Bobby Miller had given Marty or Mark a good hit, or what Gordie that was a cheap shot. Later in the game, Bobby ended up with a nice little cut up over his eye, and was told not to do those types of things to his sons. You didn't mess around with Gordie."

RAY BOURQUE
Defenseman, 1979-2001
2004 HOF Inductee

"After he finished playing, Gordie probably promoted the game -- especially in the United States -- pretty much better than anybody. He was always around a lot of the rinks, and when he was in the building, he always made his presence felt. You knew he was in the building because there was a buzz about it. He would stop by the other locker rooms, and I think he enjoyed getting to know the other guys, and getting to know the younger guys. I only met him a handful of times, but he was always a gentleman to me. He's a great ambassador for the game."

JOE MULLEN
Right wing, 1979-97
2000 HOF Inductee

"I saw him play when I was a kid, so I was pretty impressed when I started to play against him. He was feared by everybody, especially a young player like me when I came into the league at 20, 21-years-old. My first souvenir from him came in my second year in the league and our coach, Claude Ruel says to me, 'Tonight, you will shadow Gordie Howe.' So, the first face-off at center ice, I'm beside him, and I don't look at him. We won the face-off and I turned around, and he cross-checked me in the back. I slid all the way into the boards. That's how he served notice to me, and that was my first meeting with him."

SERGE SAVARD
Defenseman, 1966-83
1986 HOF Inductee

"I think there's no question that Howe would still be considered by many to be the best player that ever played for his longevity and the way he played, and the way he contributed to the team. You only got to play against five tough teams; you didn't have expansion with six extra teams for a guy like Bobby Orr to play against. So when the guy is identified as the best player now, Howe didn't have an extra six teams to filter through, and later on they put more teams in the league.

"We didn't need imaginary, made-up toughness, it was there. The guys who made it, whether it was Milt Schmidt, Jimmy Horton or Henri Richard, they had it. I would say that a guy like Howe wore that label for all of us."

DICK DUFF
Left wing, 1954-72
2006 HOF Inductee

NINE

By the Numbers

TIMELINE

1945

Nov. 1	Signed a pro contract with Detroit at the age of 17.

1946

Oct. 16	Scored his first NHL goal against Turk Broda in his NHL debut, a 3-3 tie with the Toronto Maple Leafs at Olympia Stadium.
Oct. 19	Assessed his first major penalty for a fight with Toronto's Bill Ezinicki in a 6-3 loss at Maple Leaf Gardens.
Nov. 10	Production Line of Howe, Sid Abel and Ted Lindsay started their first game as a unit in a 6-3 win over the Montreal Canadiens. Howe scored a goal and assisted on a tally by Abel.
Nov. 17	Howe, Lindsay and Abel all figure in a goal for the first time, as Lindsay scores in a 5-2 win over the Chicago Blackhawks.

1947

Feb. 27	Misses the first two games of his career after suffering a gashed instep from the skate of Toronto's Bill Ezinicki in a 3-3 tie with Toronto.
Mar. 26	Made his Stanley Cup debut in a 3-2 overtime loss to Toronto at Maple Leaf Gardens.
May 20	Finishes tied for seventh with Chicago's Bill Gadsby in the Calder Trophy balloting, each garnering four votes. Toronto's Howie Meeker (49 votes) wins the award.
Dec. 17	Collects four assists in a 7-1 win at Chicago.

1948

Apr. 1	Garners first Stanley Cup point, an assist on a Pete Horeck goal in a 3-1 win over the New York Rangers at Olympia Stadium.
Apr. 4	Registers his first Stanley Cup goal against Charlie Rayner in a 4-2 win over the New York Rangers at Madison Square Garden.
Nov. 3	Played in his first NHL All-Star Game and became involved in the first fight in All-Star Game history, tangling with Toronto's Gus Mortson as the All-Stars won 3-1.
Dec. 4	Suffered knee injury a 3-2 win over the Bruins at Boston Garden. Howe underwent knee surgery Dec. 15 for a torn ligament in his right knee and missed 20 games.

1949

Jan. 29	The game's two greatest players clash in a battle of fisticuffs, as Howe and Montreal Canadiens star Maurice (Rocket) Richard drop the gloves in Detroit's 5-2 victory at the Montreal Forum.
April 22	Named to the NHL's Second All-Star Team for the first time.
Oct. 10	Played in his second NHL All-Star Game, collecting a minor penalty as the All-Stars downed Toronto 3-1.

1950

Feb. 5	Reaches the 20-goal plateau for the first time in his NHL career with a tally against Charlie Rayner in a 5-5 tie with the New York Rangers at Olympia Stadium.
Feb. 11	Records his first NHL hat-trick against Boston's Jack Gelineau, part of a career-high five-point game in a 9-4 win at Boston Garden.
Mar. 15	Reaches the 30-goal plateau for the first time in his NHL career with a tally against Bill Durnan in a 4-1 win over the Montreal Canadiens at Olympia Stadium.
Mar. 19	Records the second hat-trick of his NHL career against Toronto's Turk Broda in a 5-0 shutout of the Maple Leafs at Olympia Stadium.
Mar. 26	Production Line of Lindsay (78 points) Abel (69) and Howe (68) finish 1-2-3 in NHL scoring, just the third time in league history that linemates have accomplished this feat.
Mar. 28	Howe is seriously injured after his head crashes into the boards when he collides with Toronto's Teeder Kennedy. Howe sustains a concussion, fractures to his nose and cheekbone and a lacerated right eyeball. Surgeons drill holes through Howe's skull to relieve pressure on the brain. His family is rushed to his bedside from Saskatoon.
Apr. 23	Moments after Detroit's Stanley Cup final win over the New York Rangers, amidst cheers of "We want Howe," Howe comes to the ice in street clothes to join the presentation of Lord Stanley's mug.
Apr. 27	Named to the NHL's Second All-Star Team for the second time.
Oct. 8	Played in his third NHL All-Star Game, tallying a goal and an assist as Detroit dumped the All-Stars 7-1.
Dec. 28	Collects a career-high five assists in an 8-1 win over Montreal at Olympia Stadium.

1951

Jan. 17	Records his third NHL hat-trick against Chicago's Harry Lumley in a 4-2 win at Chicago Stadium.
Jan. 23	Records his fourth NHL hat-trick against Chicago's Harry Lumley in a 8-2 win at Chicago Stadium.
Feb. 17	Spoils the party before 15,780 on Rocket Richard night at the Montreal Forum, beating Montreal's Gerry McNeil for the game winner in a 2-1 victory to register his 100th NHL goal.
Mar. 15	Collects his 39th goal and 79th point of the season in a 4-0 win over Boston at Olympia Stadium to establish new Red Wings marks in both categories.
Mar. 17	Records his fifth NHL hat-trick against Chicago's Harry Lumley in an 8-2 win at Olympia Stadium and also reaches the 40-goal plateau for the first time.
Mar. 18	Beats Chicago's Harry Lumley in a 4-3 win at Chicago Stadium for his 83rd point of the season, breaking the NHL single-season mark of 82 established by Boston's Herbie Cain in 1943-44.
Mar. 25	Wins his first Art Ross Trophy, leading the NHL in goals (43) assists, (43) and points (86), becoming the first NHL player to top the league in all three departments since Howie Morenz of the Montreal Canadiens in 1927-28.

Player	Games	Player	Games	Player	Games	Player	Games
Alex Delvecchio	1351	Al Johnson	97	Don Luce	43	Bob Dillabough	9
Marcel Pronovost	965	Nick Mickoski	97	John Miszuk	42	Bobby Hull	9
Norm Ullman	861	Murray Oliver	97	Marc Reaume	42	Tony Licari	9
Red Kelly	815	Hank Bassen	96	Bob Wall	40	Don McLeod	9
Ted Lindsay	745	Fern Gauthier	96	Cummy Burton	37	Dunc Fisher	8
Terry Sawchuk	718	Poul Popiel	94	Hal Jackson	36	Lloyd Haddon	8
Bruce MacGregor	662	Gord (Bucky) Hollingworth	93	Tom McCarthy	36	Chuck Luksa	8
Marty Pavelich	608	Jim Conacher	91	Gus Mortson	36	Ray Neufeld	8
Warren Godfrey	518	Joe Carveth	90	Norman (Bud) Poile	36	Steve Alley	7
Gary Bergman	466	Lee Fogolin Sr.	87	Al Dewsbury	34	John Mowers	7
Metro Prystai	426	Leo Boivin	84	Rod Morrison	34	M.F. Schurman	7
Bob Goldham	406	Albert (Junior) Langlois	82	Clare Raglan	33	Gerry Ehman	6
Val Fonteyne	370	Pete Mahovlich	82	Bill Collins	32	Guyle Fielder	6
Sid Abel	359	Pat Lundy	81	Bernie Johnston	32	Gerry Gray	6
Parker MacDonald	353	Rene Leclerc	80	Jean-Guy Talbot	32	Rick Hodgson	6
Floyd Smith	345	Gordie Roberts	80	Jim Warner	32	Marty Howe	6
Vic Stasiuk	324	Mike Rogers	80	Bob Bailey	31	Gary Marsh	6
Pete Goegan	323	Blaine Stoughton	80	Al Smith	30	Cliff Simpson	6
Bill Gadsby	322	Jordy Douglas	77	Irv Spencer	30	Ed Stankiewicz	6
Leo Reise Jr.	318	Jim Watson	77	Andre Lacroix	30	Mike Antonovich	5
Roger Crozier	312	Ed Bruneteau	76	Len (Comet) Haley	28	Ian Cushenan	5
Johnny Wilson	297	Dave Keon	76	Rick McCann	28	John Hendrickson	5
Glen Skov	295	Al Sims	76	Jim Rutherford	28	Calum Mackay	5
Tony Leswick	282	Jim (Red Eye) Hay	75	Larry Zeidel	28	Steve Wochy	5
Earl (Dutch) Reibel	271	Doug McCaig	75	Ray Cullen	27	Doug Baldwin	4
Paul Henderson	268	Mark Howe	74	Murray Costello	27	Gary Doak	4
Ben Woit	256	Nick Fotiu	74	Alan Hangsleben	27	Hugh Millar	4
Bill Dineen	255	Ed Joyal	74	Larry Brown	26	Dennis Olson	4
Billy McNeill	251	Gary Jarrett	72	Lloyd (Red) Doran	26	Stuart Smith	4
Doug Barkley	246	Greg Carroll	71	Bob McCord	26	Art Stratton	4
Nick Libett	236	Leo Labine	71	Ron Plumb	26	Bob Stephenson	4
Dean Prentice	229	Carl Brewer	70	Ron Anderson	25	Gilles Boisvert	3
Howie Young	228	Charlie Burns	70	Bill Bennett	24	Jeff Brubaker	3
(Black) Jack Stewart	219	Jim Morrison	70	George Gardner	24	Bo Elik	3
Harry Lumley	213	Steve Black	69	Billy Harris	24	Dave Gatherum	3
Garry Unger	206	Larry Hillman	69	Don McKenny	24	Roger Lafreniere	3
Len Lunde	204	John McKenzie	69	Tom Miller	24	Bill McCreary	3
Gerry (Doc) Couture	201	Hank Monteith	69	Chuck Holmes	23	Howie Menard	3
Jim McFadden	198	Reg Sinclair	69	Lou Jankowski	23	Wayne Muloin	3
Frank Mahovlich	189	Gaye Stewart	67	John MacMillan	23	Butch Paul	3
Ron Harris	181	Rick Ley	65	Keith Allen	22	Bob Perreault	3
George Gee	173	Ray Allison	64	Adam Brown	22	Thain Simon	3
Billy Dea	171	Tom Webster	63	Arnie Brown	22	Sandy Snow	3
Pete Stemkowski	170	Bart Crashley	61	Tim Ecclestone	22	Dave Amadio	2
Larry Jeffrey	169	Fred Glover	61	Ed Hatoum	21	Doug Harvey	2
Jimmy Peters Sr.	163	Don Poile	60	Lou Marcon	21	Randy Manery	2
Forbes Kennedy	162	Roy Conacher	58	Larry Wilson	21	Mike McMahon	2
Bob Baun	158	Armand (Bep) Guidolin	58	Noel Price	20	Carl Wetzel	2
Roy Edwards	158	Al Karlander	58	Tom Rowe	20	Gerry Abel	1
Bert Marshall	154	Ron Murphy	58	Gordon (Red) Berenson	19	Ralph (Red) Almas	1
Glenn Hall	148	Dale Rolfe	58	Guy Charron	19	Craig Cameron	1
Al Arbour	143	Billy Taylor	58	Lorne Davis	19	Dwight Carruthers	1
Bill Quackenbush	140	Brian Smith	57	Brian Hill	19	Harrison Gray	1
Jack McIntyre	139	Pete Babando	55	Mike Robitaille	19	Dwight Carruthers	1
Wayne Connelly	136	Ab McDonald	55	Leo Gravelle	18	Harrison Gray	1
Gerry Odrowski	132	Marc Boileau	54	Dennis Riggin	18	Galen Head	1
Andy Bathgate	129	Jimmy Peters Jr.	54	Mickey Redmond	17	Earl Johnson	1
Jerry Melnyk	127	Gerry Hart	53	Jim Niekamp	16	Brian Kilrea	1
Pete Horeck	126	Don Morrison	53	Jim Shires	14	Real Lemieux	1
Claude Laforge	120	John Garrett	52	Dale Anderson	13	Dave Lucas	1
Andre Pronovost	119	Garry Monahan	51	Murray Hall	13	Lou Marcon	1
Bryan (Bugsy) Watson	117	Barry Cullen	50	Jim Krulicki	13	Tom McGrattan	1
Clare Martin	114	Doug Roberts	50	Mark Renaud	13	Bill Mitchell	1
Gary Aldcorn	113	Gord Strate	50	Gene Achtymichuk	12	Eddie Nicholson	1
Max McNab	113	Ron Ingram	49	Les Douglas	12	David Richardson	1
Pit Martin	109	Dave Debol	48	Bill Folk	12	Dave Rochefort	1
Ted Hampson	108	Bob Falkenberg	48	Tim Sheehy	12	Pat Rupp	1
Kent Douglas	105	Pat Boutette	47	Ed Diachuk	11	Jean Savard	1
John Bucyk	104	Larry Giroux	47	Hec Lalande	11	Bob Solinger	1
Marcel Bonin	101	Serge Lajeunesse	47	Gary Croteau	10	Thain Simon	1
Lorne Ferguson	101	Jim (Enio) Sclisizzi	47	Stu McNeill	10	Ted Taylor	1
Alex Faulkner	99	Lowell MacDonald	46	Fred Speck	10	Doug Volmar	1
Howie Glover	99	Danny Lawson	45	Johnny Brenneman	9	Ross (Lefty) Wilson	1

1951 continued

Apr. 18	Named co-winner of The Hockey News player-of-the-year award with Maurice (Rocket) Richard of the Montreal Canadiens.
Apr. 28	Named to the NHL's First All-Star Team for the first time.
Oct. 9	Played in his fourth NHL All-Star Game, scoring for the First All-Star Team as they tied the Second Team 2-2 at Toronto's Maple Leaf Gardens.
Dec. 31	Records his sixth NHL hat-trick against Montreal's Gerry McNeil in a 5-3 loss to the Canadiens at Olympia Stadium.

1952

Mar. 8	Beats Toronto's Al Rollins in a 6-3 loss at Maple Leaf Gardens to join Montreal's Maurice (Rocket) Richard as the only players in NHL history to record back-to-back 40-goal seasons.
Mar. 20	Scores his 44th goal of the season against Lorne Anderson of the New York Rangers in a 7-3 win at Olympia Stadium to shatter his own club record for goals in a season.
Mar. 23	Wins his second straight Art Ross Trophy, tying his own club record with 86 points and establishing a new team mark with 47 goals. Also records his seventh NHL hat-trick against Montreal's Gerry McNeil in a 7-2 win at Olympia Stadium.
Apr. 15	Detroit completes back-to-back series sweeps with a 3-0 shutout of the Montreal Canadiens as Howe captures his second Stanley Cup, sharing the playoff scoring lead with seven points.
Apr. 22	Named to the NHL's First All-Star Team for the second time.
May 1	Won the Hart Trophy as MVP of the NHL for the first time.
Oct. 5	Played in his fifth NHL All-Star Game as Howe's First Team All-Stars tied 1-1 with the Second Team at Olympia Stadium.

1953

Jan. 11	Records his eighth NHL hat-trick against Toronto's Harry Lumley in a 5-2 win at Olympia Stadium.
Jan. 29	Records his ninth NHL hat-trick against Chicago's Al Rollins in a 5-2 win at Chicago Stadium.
Feb. 1	Equals career high with five points in a 5-1 win over Toronto at Olympia Stadium.
Feb. 15	Beats Chicago's Al Rollins in a 4-1 win at Chicago Stadium to record goal No. 200 of his NHL career. It's also his 40th goal of the season, making Howe the first player in NHL history to record three straight 40-goal campaigns.
Mar. 5	Equals career high with five points in a 7-1 win over the New York Rangers at Olympia Stadium. His assist on a goal by Red Kelly sets a new NHL record for points in a season with 87, while his final point of the night, an assist on a goal by Ted Lindsay, makes Howe the first player in NHL history to record 90 points in a season. Also beats Gump Worsley of the New York Rangers on the first penalty shot of his NHL career.
Mar. 22	Wins his third straight Art Ross Trophy, becoming the first player to lead the league in scoring three years in a row. He registered a league-record 95 points with a Wings' record 49 goals, and tied a club mark with 46 assists.
Apr. 15	Wed the former Colleen Joffa at Detroit's Calvary Presbyterian Church.
Apr. 24	Named to the NHL's First All-Star Team for the third time.
Apr. 27	Named The Hockey News player of the year.
May 4	Won the Hart Trophy as MVP of the NHL for the second time.
Oct. 3	Played in his sixth NHL All-Star Game as the All-Stars downed Montreal 3-1.
Oct. 11	Scored a goal, garnered two assists and fought Fern Flaman to record the first Gordie Howe hat-trick of his career in a 4-0 shutout of Toronto at Olympia Stadium.

1954

Feb. 14	Records his 500th point, an assist on a goal by Ted Lindsay in a 3-0 win over Montreal at Olympia Stadium.
Mar. 21	Wins his NHL-record fourth Art Ross Trophy in succession, setting a Wings club record with 48 assists.
Apr. 1	Just nine-seconds into the game -- a 4-3 win over Toronto at Olympia Stadium -- Howe sets a Stanley Cup record for the fastest goal.
Apr. 16	Howe wins his third Stanley Cup when the Wings secure a 2-1 overtime win over Montreal in Game 7 of the final series at Olympia Stadium.
Apr. 23	Named to the NHL's First All-Star Team for the fourth time.
Oct. 3	Played in his seventh NHL All-Star Game, scoring once as Detroit and the All-Stars tied 2-2.
Nov. 3	Suffers a shoulder injury in a 1-1 tie at Toronto and misses six games, ending his consecutive games played streak at 382.
Dec. 1	Beat Johnny Bower of the New York Rangers in a 6-1 win at Madison Square Garden to become the sixth player in NHL history to reach the 250-goal plateau.

1955

Jan. 27	In a game against the Rangers, Howe's younger brother, Vic, steals the show by scoring the game-tying goal against the Red Wings at 11:57 of the third period.
Mar. 3	Records his 10th hat-trick in a 6-1 win over Chicago at Olympia Stadium.
Apr. 10	Records his first playoff hat-trick against Montreal's Jacques Plante in a 5-1 win over the Canadiens in Game 5 of the Stanley Cup final at Olympia Stadium.
Apr. 14	Scored the Stanley Cup-winning goal as Detroit downed Montreal 3-1 in Game 7 of the final series at Olympia Stadium. While winning his fourth Stanley Cup, Howe established a playoff record with 20 points, a mark that would stand until 1970.
Oct. 2	Played in his eighth NHL All-Star Game, collecting a goal and an assist as Detroit beat the All-Stars 3-1.

Gordie's Playoff Teamates

Player	Games	Player	Games	Player	Games	Player	Games
Alex Delvecchio	121	Pit Martin	17	Gaye Stewart	6	Bobby Hull	3
Marcel Pronovost	109	Jimmy Peters Sr.	17	Keith Allen	5	Bernie Johnston	3
Ted Lindsay	92	Marcel Bonin	16	Ralph (Red) Almas	5	Dave Keon	3
Terry Sawchuk	84	Len Lunde	16	Roy Conacher	5	Clare Martin	3
Red Kelly	82	Max McNab	16	Doug McCaig	5	John Miszuk	3
Norm Ullman	80	John Bucyk	15	Ron Murphy	5	Don Morrison	3
Marty Pavelich	75	Lorne Ferguson	15	Brian Smith	5	Rod Morrison	3
Bruce MacGregor	56	Glenn Hall	15	Billy Taylor	5	Gordie Roberts	3
Bob Goldham	53	Irv Spencer	15	Larry Zeidel	5	Mike Rogers	3
Parker MacDonald	50	Jim Conacher	14	Hank Bassen	4	Tom Rowe	3
Bill Gadsby	44	Pat Lundy	14	Bobby Baun	4	Al Sims	3
Metro Prystai	43	Al Arbour	13	Carl Brewer	4	Ray Allison	2
Glen Skov	43	Fern Gauthier	13	Wayne Connelly	4	Reg Sinclair	2
Floyd Smith	43	Larry Hillman	13	Murray Costello	4	Dale Anderson	2
Johnny Wilson	42	Jim (Enio) Sclisizzi	13	Barry Cullen	4	Joe Dube	2
Tony Leswick	41	Andy Bathgate	12	Roy Edwards	4	Bep Guidolin	2
Ben Woit	41	Leo Boivin	12	Guyle Fielder	4	Murray Hall	2
Vic Stasiuk	40	Alex Faulkner	12	Fred Glover	4	Steve Hrymnak	2
Sid Abel	38	Lee Fogolin Sr.	12	Ron Harris	4	John McKenzie	2
Bill Dineen	37	Bert Marshall	12	Al Karlander	4	Ray Neufeld	2
Earl (Dutch) Reibel	35	Gerry Odrowski	12	Forbes Kennedy	4	Marc Reaume	2
Warren Godfrey	34	Dean Prentice	12	Nick Libett	4	Gerry Reid	2
Pete Goegan	33	Bryan (Bugsy) Watson	12	John MacMillan	4	Cliff Simpson	2
Paul Henderson	33	Howie Glover	11	Frank Mahovlich	4	Al Smith	2
Leo Reise Jr.	33	Al Johnson	11	Billy McNeill	4	Doug Volmar	2
Ed Joyal	32	Leo Labine	11	Nick Mickoski	4	Pete Babando	1
Doug Barkley	30	Ed Bruneteau	10	Hank Monteith	4	Steve Black	1
Jim McFadden	29	Ab MacDonald	10	Don Poile	4	Joe Carveth	1
Pete Horeck	26	Jack McIntyre	10	Dale Rolfe	4	Bob Champoux	1
Bill Quackenbush	26	Norman (Bud) Poile	10	Pete Stemkowski	4	John Garrett	1
(Black) Jack Stewart	26	Bob Bailey	9	Garry Unger	4	Lloyd Haddon	1
Larry Jeffrey	25	Billy Dea	9	Steve Alley	3	Rick Hodgson	1
Andre Pronovost	25	Jim (Red Eye) Hay	9	Pat Boutette	3	Lou Jankowski	1
Jerry Melnyk	23	Nellie Podlosky	7	Cummy Burton	3	Lowell MacDonald	1
Roger Crozier	22	Bob Wall	7	Dave Debol	3	Hugh Millar	1
Harry Lumley	22	Gary Aldcorn	6	Al Dewsbury	3	John Mowers	1
Gary Bergman	21	Bob Dillabough	6	Nick Fotiu	3	Poul Popiel	1
Albert (Junior) Langlois	20	Val Fonteyne	6	Larry Giroux	3	Blaine Stoughton	1
Howie Young	19	Len (Comet) Haley	6	Gord (Bucky) Hollingworth	3		
Gerry (Doc) Couture	18	Jim Morrison	6	Mark Howe	3		
George Gee	17	Murray Oliver	6	Marty Howe	3		

TIMELINE

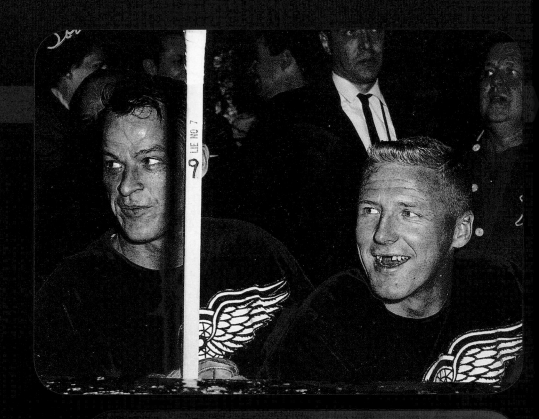

1956

Jan. 19	Records his 11th NHL hat-trick against Boston's Terry Sawchuk in a 4-2 win over the Bruins at Olympia Stadium.
Feb. 7	Beat Chicago's Al Rollins in a 2-2 tie at Olympia Stadium to become the third NHL player to register 300 goals.
Apr. 16	Named to the NHL's Second All-Star Team for the third time.
Dec. 15	Beat the Blackhawks' Al Rollins in a 2-1 win at Olympia Stadium to register goal No. 325, passing Nels Stewart for second place on the all-time list.
Dec. 25	Collected a career-high six points in a 6-1 win over the Rangers and goalie Gump Worsley at Olympia Stadium, including the 12th hat-trick of his NHL career.

1957

Apr. 22	Named to the NHL's First All-Star Team for the fifth time
Apr. 27	Named The Hockey News player of the year.
May 4	Won the Hart Trophy as MVP of the NHL for the third time.
Oct. 5	Played in his ninth NHL All-Star Game, scoring the game-winner as the All-Stars downed the Canadiens 5-3.

1958

Jan. 25	Suffered two broken ribs in a 5-3 loss at Boston Garden and missed five games.
Apr. 28	Named to the NHL's First All-Star Team for the sixth time.
May 12	Won the Hart Trophy as MVP of the NHL for a record-tying fourth time.
Oct. 4	Played in his 10th NHL All-Star Game, as the All-Stars fell 6-3 to the Canadiens.
Dec. 13	Beat Jacques Plante in a 2-2 tie with the Canadiens at the Montreal Forum for goal No. 400.

1959

Feb. 1	During a 5-4 loss to the Rangers, Howe badly fractures the nose of defenseman Lou Fontinato, who at the time was considered the NHL's best fighter, in a bout at Madison Square Garden.
Mar. 3	On "Gordie Howe Night" at Olympia Stadium, Howe is feted with over $10,000 in gifts, including a new station wagon with the licence plate GH-9000. When the door of the car is opened, Howe's parents, Ab and Katherine, step out of the car.
Apr. 27	Named to the NHL's Second All-Star Team for the fourth time.
June 12	Named captain of the Red Wings.
Oct. 3	Played in his 11th NHL All-Star Game, as the All-Stars dropped a 6-1 decision to the Canadiens.

1960

Jan. 13	Scores a goal in a 5-2 loss to the Blackhawks to tie Rocket Richard (945 points) for first on the NHL's career scoring list.
Jan. 16	Assists on a goal by Alex Delvecchio in a 3-1 win over the Blackhawks at Olympia Stadium to become the NHL's career scoring leader.
Apr. 22	Named to the NHL's First All-Star Team for the seventh time.
Apr. 24	Named The Hockey News player of the year.
May 4	Won the Hart Trophy as MVP of the NHL for a record fifth time.
Oct. 1	Playing in his 12th NHL All-Star Game, Howe suffers a knee injury in a 2-1 win over the Canadiens; misses the first two games of the regular-season.
Nov. 27	Set-up Norm Ullman for a goal in a 2-0 win over Toronto at Olympia Stadium to become the NHL's first player to reach 1,000-points.
Dec. 1	Assisting on a goal by Murray Oliver in a 3-2 loss to the Bruins at Boston Garden moves Howe past Rocket Richard (1,091) as the NHL's career-leader in combined regular-season and playoff points.

1961

Jan. 4	Suffered a concussion and a large cut to the forehead when hit by Toronto's Eddie Shack in a 6-4 loss at Maple Leaf Gardens; missed next four games.
Dec. 18	Set a new NHL record with his 84th game-winning goal in a 3-1 victory over the Canadiens at the Montreal Forum.
Feb. 5	Began a streak of recording a point in 18 consecutive games which ended on March 15. A new club record.
Mar. 15	Set a new NHL record for right-wingers by recording his 49th assist of the season in a 2-2 tie at Chicago Stadium.
April 8	Collected two assists in a 3-1 Detroit win over Chicago in Game 2 of the Stanley Cup final to move past Doug Harvey (59) and become the NHL's all-time leader in playoff assists.
Apr. 16	Shared the Stanley Cup scoring lead with 15 points.
Apr. 23	Named to the NHL's Second All-Star Team for the fifth time.
Oct. 7	Played in his 13th NHL All-Star Game, collecting a goal and an assist as the All-Stars down the Blackhawks 3-1.
Dec. 31	Records his 13th NHL hat-trick against Toronto's Johnny Bower in a 4-3 win at Olympia Stadium.

1962

Mar. 14	Beat Gump Worsley in a 3-2 loss to New York at Madison Square Garden to become the second player in NHL history to register 500 goals.
Apr. 30	Named to the NHL's Second All-Star Team for the sixth time.
Sep. 4	Accepted an assistant coaching position with the Wings and relinquished the team captaincy to Alex Delvecchio.
Oct. 6	Played in his record-setting 14th NHL All-Star Game, scoring the only goal as the All-Stars drop a 4-1 decision to the Maple Leafs.

Teamate's Regular Season Assists

Player	Games	Player	Games	Player	Games	Player	Games
Alex Delvecchio	210	Gary Jarrett	6	Leo Boivin	2	Gerry (Doc) Couture	1
Ted Lindsay	147	Ed Litzenberger	6	Bill Collins	2	Dave Debol	1
Norm Ullman	88	Ron Murphy	6	Bart Crashley	2	Lloyd (Red) Doran	1
Red Kelly	84	Don Poile	6	Ray Cullen	2	Tim Ecclestone	1
Sid Abel	65	Floyd Smith	6	Billy Dea	2	Lorne Ferguson	1
Marcel Pronovost	45	Kent Douglas	5	Ted Hampson	2	George Gee	1
Frank Mahovlich	40	Bruce MacGregor	5	Alan Hangsleben	2	Ron Ingram	1
Parker MacDonald	39	Bert Marshall	5	Paul Henderson	2	Dave Keon	1
Earl (Dutch) Reibel	39	Andre Pronovost	5	Bernie Johnston	2	Forbes Kennedy	1
Gary Bergman	20	Mike Rogers	5	Al Karlander	2	Andre Lacroix	1
Johnny Wilson	19	Glen Skov	5	Don Luce	2	Albert (Junior) Langlois	1
Bob Goldham	18	(Black) Jack Stewart	5	John MacMillan	2	Danny Lawson	1
Metro Prystai	18	Tom Webster	5	Pete Mahovlich	2	Rick Ley	1
Dean Prentice	17	Al Arbour	4	Pit Martin	2	Nick Libett	1
Vic Stasiuk	15	Joe Carveth	4	Tom McCarthy	2	Pat Lundy	1
Bill Gadsby	12	Bill Dineen	4	Jim McFadden	2	Clare Martin	1
Marty Pavelich	12	Ed Joyal	4	Don McKenny	2	Ab McDonald	1
Leo Reise Jr.	12	Carl Brewer	3	Gerry Odrowski	2	Jerry Melnyk	1
Howie Young	11	John Bucyk	3	Jimmy Peters Jr.	2	Tom Miller	1
Warren Godfrey	10	Charlie Burns	3	Norman (Bud) Poile	2	Jim Niekamp	1
Jack McIntyre	10	Lee Fogolin Sr.	3	Poul Popiel	2	Bill Quackenbush	1
Murray Oliver	10	Val Fonteyne	3	Al Sims	2	Matt Ravlich	1
Gary Aldcorn	9	Gerry Hart	3	Ray Allison	1	Gordie Roberts	1
Doug Barkley	9	Jim (Red Eye) Hay	3	Keith Allen	1	Mike Robitaille	1
Andy Bathgate	9	Larry Hillman	3	Mike Antonovich	1	Terry Sawchuk	1
Len Lunde	9	Gord (Bucky) Hollingworth	3	Gordon (Red) Berenson	1	Reg Sinclair	1
Garry Unger	9	Mark Howe	3	Marc Boileau	1	Brian Smith	1
Pete Goegan	8	Claude Laforge	3	John Brenneman	1	Art Stratton	1
Ron Harris	8	Billy McNeill	3	Adam Brown	1	Jean-Guy Talbot	1
Jim Morrison	8	Nick Mickoski	3	Arnie Brown	1	Bob Wall	1
Bob Baun	7	Dale Rolfe	3	Greg Carroll	1	Bryan (Bugsy) Watson	1
Doug Roberts	7	Pete Stemkowski	2	Real Chevrefils	1	Larry Wilson	1
Wayne Connelly	6	Hank Bassen	2	Jim Conacher	1	Ben Woit	1

Gordie's Regular Season Assists

Player	Games	Player	Games	Player	Games	Player	Games
Alex Delvecchio	183	Bill Gadsby	6	Real Chevrefils	2	Leo Gravelle	1
Ted Lindsay	142	Glen Skov	6	Jim Conacher	2	Ron Harris	1
Norm Ullman	88	Doug Roberts	6	Lorne Ferguson	2	Larry Hillman	1
Sid Abel	52	Mike Rogers	6	George Gee	2	Gord (Bucky) Hollingworth	1
Frank Mahovlich	52	Tom Webster	6	Howie Glover	2	Lou Jankowski	1
Red Kelly	48	Billy Dea	5	Ted Hampson	2	Al Johnson	1
Parker MacDonald	46	Jordy Douglas	5	Mark Howe	2	Ed Joyal	1
Earl (Dutch) Reibel	30	Claude Laforge	5	Dave Keon	2	Leo Labine	1
Murray Oliver	20	Jerry Melnyk	5	Lowell MacDonald	2	Andre Lacroix	1
Metro Prystai	16	Don Poile	5	Jim Morrison	2	Rick Ley	1
Gary Bergman	15	Joe Carveth	4	Jimmy Peters Jr.	2	Clare Martin	1
Jack McIntyre	14	Les Douglas	4	(Black) Jack Stewart	2	Pit Martin	1
Marcel Pronovost	14	Val Fonteyne	4	Howie Young	2	Doug McCaig	1
Vic Stasiuk	14	Fred Glover	4	Ray Allison	1	Tom McCarthy	1
Johnny Wilson	14	Larry Jeffrey	4	Al Arbour	1	Bob McCord	1
Ron Murphy	12	Nick Libett	4	Bill Bennett	1	Ab McDonald	1
Paul Henderson	11	Andre Pronovost	4	Gordon (Red) Berenson	1	John McKenzie	1
Bruce MacGregor	10	Bill Quackenbush	4	Marc Boileau	1	Billy McNeill	1
Floyd Smith	10	Pete Stemkowski	4	Leo Boivin	1	Nick Mickoski	1
Garry Unger	10	Andy Bathgate	3	Marcel Bonin	1	Ron Plumb	1
Gary Aldcorn	9	Ray Cullen	3	Adam Brown	1	Mike Robitaille	1
Dean Prentice	9	Nick Fotiu	3	Arnie Brown	1	Tim Sheehy	1
Bill Dineen	8	Rene Leclerc	3	Guy Charron	1	Al Sims	1
Pete Goegan	8	Ed Litzenberger	3	Roy Conacher	1	Irv Spencer	1
Len Lunde	8	Jim McFadden	3	Gerry (Doc) Couture	1	Blaine Stoughton	1
Warren Godfrey	7	Max McNab	3	Al Dewsbury	1	Bob Wall	1
Marty Pavelich	7	Leo Reise Jr.	3	Fern Gauthier	1	Ben Woit	1
Doug Barkley	6	Billy Taylor	3	Bob Goldham	1		

1962 continued

Nov. 24	Became the first player to skate in 1,000 NHL games as Detroit tied the Blackhawks 1-1 at Chicago Stadium.

1963

Mar. 24	Won the Art Ross Trophy as NHL scoring champion for a record sixth time.
Apr. 13	Named The Hockey News player of the year.
Apr. 18	Shared the NHL playoff scoring lead with 16 points.
Apr. 26	Named to the NHL's First All-Star Team for the eighth time.
May 9	Won the Hart Trophy as MVP of the NHL for an unprecedented sixth time.
Oct. 6	Played in his 15th NHL All-Star Game, garnering an assist as the All-Stars gained a 3-3 tie with the Maple Leafs.
Oct. 27	Recorded goal No. 544 to tie Rocket Richard for the NHL's all-time lead in a 6-4 loss to the Canadiens at Montreal Forum.
Nov. 10	Becomes the NHL's all-time goal scoring leader when he beats Charlie Hodge for No. 545 with a shorthanded goal in a 3-0 win over the Canadiens at Olympia Stadium.
Dec. 29	Beat Boston's Ed Johnston in a 2-1 win over the Bruins at Olympia Stadium to become the first NHL player to score 600 combined regular-season and playoff goals.

1964

Mar. 26	Howe and Wings teammate Red Kelly set an NHL record by participating in their 16th Stanley Cup playoff.
Apr. 5	His goal in a 3-1 loss to the Blackhawks at Chicago Stadium moved Howe past Rocket Richard (126 points) as the career scoring leader in Stanley Cup history.
Apr. 30	Named to the NHL's Second All-Star Team for the seventh time.
Oct. 6	Played in his 16th NHL All-Star Game, collecting an assist as the All-Stars edged the Maple Leafs 3-2.
Nov. 14	Beat Charlie Hodge in a 4-2 loss to the Canadiens at the Montreal Forum to surpass Rocket Richard's combined NHL mark for regular-season and playoff goals of 626.
Dec. 16	Ended a career-high 12-game goal-scoring slump by beating Jacques Plante twice in a 7-3 win over the Rangers at Madison Square Garden.

1965

Mar. 21	Records his 14th NHL hat-trick against Chicago's Denis DeJordy in a 5-1 win over the Blackhawks at Olympia Stadium.
May 6	Named to the NHL's Second All-Star Team for the eighth time.
Oct. 6	Played in his 17th NHL All-Star Game, garnering a game-record four points to earn MVP honors as the All-Stars drubbed the Canadiens 5-2. Howe also established an All-Star Game career mark by scoring his eighth All-Star goal.
Oct. 23	Playing in an 8-1 loss to the Canadiens at the Montreal Forum, Howe and Wings teammate Bill Gadsby join former Bruins great Dit Clapper as the only players to skate in 20 NHL seasons.
Nov. 27	In a 3-2 loss to the Canadiens at Montreal Forum, Howe beat Gump Worsley for career goal No. 600.
Dec. 12	Records his 15th NHL hat-trick against Boston's Gerry Cheevers in a 5-3 win at Boston Garden.

1966

Feb. 4	Playing at Boston Garden despite receiving an anonymous letter threatening his life, Howe reaches the 20-goal plateau for the 17th successive season as the Wings beat the Bruins 4-2.
May 12	Named to the NHL's First All-Star Team for the ninth time.
July 22	Thousands of people line the city streets in Howe's hometown of Saskatoon, which declares it 'Gordie Howe Day'. He is honored with a parade, a civic reception and an evening tribute program.
Oct. 14	As part of their 30th anniversary celebration, The Hockey News name Howe the top NHL player of the past 20 seasons.
Oct. 19	Playing in a 6-2 season-opening loss to the Bruins at Boston Garden, Howe sets an NHL record by skating in his 21st season.

1967

Jan. 18	Played in his 18th NHL All-Star Game as the Montreal Canadiens blanked the All-Stars 3-0.
Jan. 26	Awarded the Lester Patrick Trophy for outstanding contribution to hockey in the U.S.
May 10	Named to the NHL's Second All-Star Team for the ninth time.

1968

Jan. 16	Played in his 19th NHL All-Star Game and collected an assist and a roughing penalty for tangling with Mike Walton as the All-Stars fell 4-3 to the Maple Leafs.
May 16	Named to the NHL's First All-Star Team for the 10th time.
Dec. 4	Beat Pittsburgh goalie Les Binkley in a 7-2 win at Pittsburgh's Civic Arena to become the first NHL player to score 700 goals.

1969

Jan. 21	Played in his 20th NHL All-Star Game as the East and West Divisions skated to a 3-3 tie in Montreal.
Mar. 30	Beat Denis DeJordy in a 9-5 win over the Blackhawks at Chicago Stadium to become the first player in Red Wings history to record a 100-point season.
May 8	Named to the NHL's First All-Star Team for the 11th time.

Teamate's Playoff Assists

Player	Assists	Player	Assists	Player	Assists	Player	Assists
Alex Delvecchio	21	Floyd Smith	4	Bob Goldham	1	Metro Prystai	1
Ted Lindsay	12	Bill Gadsby	3	Larry Hillman	1	Bill Quackenbush	1
Norm Ullman	10	Vic Stasiuk	3	Mark Howe	1	Leo Reise Jr.	1
Red Kelly	6	George Gee	2	Bruce MacGregor	1	Johnny Wilson	1
Marcel Pronovost	5	Larry Jeffrey	2	Bert Marshall	1	Ben Woit	1
Sid Abel	4	Doug Barkley	1	Jack McIntyre	1	Howie Young	1
Parker MacDonald	4	Wayne Connelly	1	Marty Pavelich	1		
Earl Reibel	4	Warren Godfrey	1	Norman (Bud) Poile	1		

Gordie's Playoff Assists

Player	Assists	Player	Assists	Player	Assists	Player	Assists
Ted Lindsay	20	Larry Jeffrey	2	George Gee	1	Jerry Melnyk	1
Alex Delvecchio	19	Red Kelly	2	Bob Goldham	1	Ray Neufeld	1
Parker MacDonald	6	Len Lunde	2	Pete Horeck	1	Murray Oliver	1
Norm Ullman	6	Jack McIntyre	2	Al Johnson	1	Marty Pavelich	1
Sid Abel	5	Dean Prentice	2	Ed Joyal	1	Leo Reise Jr.	1
Earl Reibel	3	Floyd Smith	2	Leo Labine	1	Ben Woit	1
Vic Stasiuk	3	Billy Dea	1	Bruce MacGregor	1		
Andy Bathgate	2	Alex Faulkner	1	Pit Martin	1		

TIMELINE

1970

Jan. 20	Played in his 21st NHL All-Star Game, scoring the game winner, his 10th goal in All-Star play, as the East downed the West 4-1 in St. Louis.
Apr. 5	Finished ninth in NHL scoring with a team-leading 71 points, marking the first time in 21 seasons that Howe doesn't finish among the NHL's top five scorers.
Apr. 12	Played in his 154th and final Stanley Cup game as a Red Wing, scoring on Blackhawks goalie Tony Esposito in a 4-2 loss to Chicago at Olympia Stadium.
May 21	Named to the NHL's First All-Star Team for the 12th time.
May 25	Howe is honored with 'Gordie Howe Day' in Windsor, Ontario.
May 27	Underwent surgery at the University of Michigan Medical Center for removal of loose bone fragments and a dead navicular bone in his left wrist.
Oct. 15	Six games into the season, Wings coach Ned Harkness ends the experiment of Howe as a defenseman and returned him to right wing.
Nov. 24	Suffered fractured ribs in a 4-2 win over Philadelphia and missed 10 games.

1971

Jan. 19	Played in his 22nd NHL All-Star Game as the East fell 2-1 to the West in Boston.
Feb. 22	Suffering from the flu and chronic wrist pain, Howe is sent to Florida to recuperate and missed five games.
Feb. 24	Howe is awarded the Medal of Service of the Order of Canada.
Mar. 31	Collected his 1,023rd and final assist in a 2-2 tie at Maple Leaf Gardens. The Leafs presented Howe with a silver tea service in honor of his 43rd birthday and the capacity crowd afforded him a one-minute standing ovation.
Apr. 3	In his farewell regular-season game at Olympia Stadium, Howe scores goal No. 786, coming against Chicago's Tony Esposito in a 4-1 loss to the Blackhawks.
Sept. 8	After a record 25 seasons in Detroit, Howe announces his retirement as a player.

> *It wasn't very pleasant playing against him, because he was a great player. It's more fun playing against bums, you know, but there was no fun playing against him, I'll tell you. I think that Gordie Howe is in a class all of his own. There was Howe, Lindsay, Beliveau and Richard -- that's the upper echelon of great players. Gordie is in that class of player, who will forever be remembered as the best player to play in his day.*

GEORGE ARMSTRONG | Right wing, 1949-71
1975 HOF Inductee

1972

Mar. 12	In a ceremony at Olympia Stadium prior to a game against Chicago, Howe's No. 9 is retired by the Red Wings.
Jun. 7	The regular three-year waiting period is waived as Howe is inducted into the Hockey Hall of Fame.

1973

Jun. 11	Tendered his resignation as Red Wings' vice president.
Jun. 19	Ending a two-year retirement from the game, Howe joins the WHA's Houston Aeros.
Oct. 8	Howe plays his first pro game in Detroit since his NHL retirement, collecting two assists as Houston downs the Los Angeles Sharks in an exhibition game at Cobo Arena.

1974

Jan. 17	Scored his 800th professional goal as Houston defeated the Vancouver Blazers 7-4.
Mar. 18	Named WHA player of the year by The Hockey News.
May 10	Named to the WHA First All-Star Team.
May 20	Collected four assists as Houston defeated the Chicago Cougars 6-2 to win the Avco Cup title.
May 28	Howe is named MVP of the WHA.
Sep. 17	Howe is part of a WHA Team Canada squad that falls 4-1-3 to the Soviet Union in a Summit Series that concludes on Oct. 6.

1975

May 8	Named to the WHA First All-Star Team.
May 12	Scored two goals and two assists as Houston downed the Quebec Nordiques 7-2 to give Howe his second WHA Avco Cup title. He is the first player in hockey history to have won multiple Stanley Cup and Avco Cup titles.
Aug. 5	The WHA renames its MVP award the Gordie Howe Trophy.

1976

Nov. 16	Scored the 100th goal of his WHA career in a 4-2 win over the Calgary Cowboys.

1977

May 23	Howe and his sons, Mark and Marty, sign with the WHA's New England Whalers.
Dec. 7	Howe scored his 1,000th professional goal against John Garrett as New England defeated the Birmingham Bulls 6-3.

Regular Season Goaltenders Scored On

Goaltender	Goals Against	Goaltender	Goals Against	Goaltender	Goals Against	Goaltender	Goals Against
Gump Worsley	70	Gerry Cheevers	17	Doug Favell	4	Gary Inness	1
Harry Lumley	60	Don Simmons	17	Seth Martin	4	Doug Jackson	1
Jacques Plante	54	Bill Durnan	15	Wayne Rutledge	4	Julian Klymkiew	1
Al Rollins	53	Bruce Gamble	14	Al Smith	4	Mike Liut	1
Johnny Bower	48	Frank Brimsek	12	Joe Daley	3	Markus Mattsson	1
Glenn Hall	43	Gary Smith	12	Don Head	3	Gil Mayer	1
(Sugar) Jim Henry	31	Emile Francis	10	Mike Palmateer	3	Jack McCartan	1
Gerry McNeil	28	Ceasare Maniago	10	Bob Perreault	3	Al Millar	1
Ed Johnston	27	Tony Esposito	9	Lorne Anderson	2	Greg Millen	1
Terry Sawchuk	23	Les Binkley	8	Garry Bauman	2	Bill Oleschuk	1
Denis DeJordy	22	Rogatien Vachon	7	Jack Norris	2	Dan Olesevich	1
Walter (Turk) Broda	21	Marcel Paille	7	Paul Bibeault	1	Pat Riggin	1
Jack Gelineau	20	Bernie Parent	7	Ken Broderick	1	Ernie Wakely	1
Charlie Hodge	19	Gerry Desjardins	6	Roger Crozier	1	Carl Wetzel	1
Ed Giacomin	18	Hank Bassen	5	John Davidson	1	Dunc Wilson	1
Charlie Rayner	18	Dave Dryden	5	Marv Edwards	1	Empty Net	7
Ed Chadwick	17	(Long) John Henderson	5	Rob Holland	1		

Playoff Goaltenders Scored On

Goaltender	Goals Against	Goaltender	Goals Against
Glenn Hall	17	Tony Esposito	2
Johnny Bower	11	Sugar Jim Henry	2
Harry Lumley	9	Don Simmons	2
Bill Durnan	8	Denis Herron	1
Jacques Plante	8	Charlie Rayner	1
Gerry McNeil	6	Gump Worsley	1

TIMELINE

1979

Jan. 2-5   Howe and Wayne Gretzky are teammates for the only time in their careers as the WHA All-Stars sweep a three-game series from Moscow Dynamo.

Oct. 11   For the first time since 1971, Howe, 51, skates in an NHL game, playing for the Hartford Whalers in a 4-1 loss to the Minnesota North Stars at the Metropolitan Sports Center.

1980

Jan. 12   In his first NHL game in Detroit in nearly nine years, Howe receives numerous standing ovations from the Joe Louis Arena crowd of 19,905 and is named the game's first star as his Whalers beat the Wings 6-4.

Feb. 5   Playing for the Wales Conference in the NHL All-Star Game at Joe Louis Arena, his record 23rd appearance in the game, Howe is afforded a tumultuous standing ovation from the capacity crowd of 21,002, at the time the largest to ever watch a pro game. Howe collects an assist as the Wales team beat the Campbell Conference 6-3.

Feb. 21   During an occasion billed as the final hockey game at Olympia Stadium, Howe scores the last goal of the game as the Wings Oldtimers fall 6-2 to the Red Wings before 14,354.

Feb. 29   Scores his 800th NHL goal for Hartford against Mike Liut and the St. Louis Blues in a 3-0 win.

Apr. 6   In a 5-3 win over the Red Wings at Hartford, Howe registers the final points of his NHL regular-season career - his 801st goal and his 1,049th assist.

Jun. 4   For the second time in his NHL career, Howe announces his retirement from the game.

1981

Feb. 9   The Whalers retired Howe's No. 9 sweater prior to a game against Winnipeg.

1982

July 7   Named special assistant to Hartford managing general partner Howard Baldwin.

1984

Nov. 22   Inducted into the Red Wings' Hall of Fame.

2006

Nov. 22   The West Entrance to Joe Louis Arena is renamed the Gordie Howe Entrance.

2007

Apr. 10   A statue of Howe commissioned by the Wings and created by artist Omri Amrany is unveiled outside the West Entrance to Joe Louis Arena.

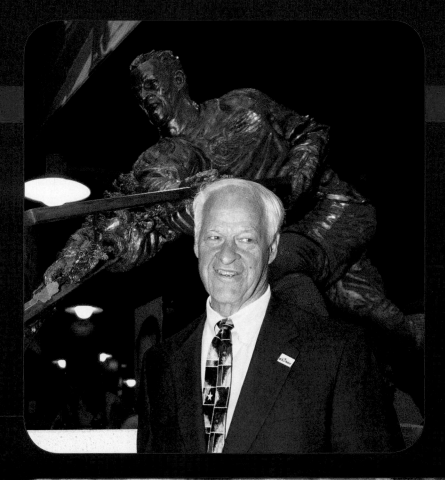

Arena (Team)	GP	G	A	PTS	PIM
Olympia Stadium (Detroit)	844	439	604	1043	858
Chicago Stadium (Chicago)	152	76	75	151	152
Madison Square Garden (NY Rangers)	143	57	91	148	145
Boston Garden (Boston)	159	65	77	142	146
Maple Leaf Gardens (Toronto)	155	55	71	126	142
Montreal Forum (Montreal)	158	59	66	125	160
Hartford Civic Center (Hartford)	40	7	15	22	32
St. Louis Arena (St. Louis)	15	6	9	15	8
The Forum (Los Angeles)	13	7	6	13	6
The Spectrum (Philadelphia)	12	5	8	13	6
Met Center (Minnesota)	12	5	7	12	0
Madison Square Garden (NY Rangers)*	13	5	4	9	6
Oakland Coliseum (Oakland)	10	4	5	9	4
Civic Arena (Pittsburgh)	13	6	2	8	10
Memorial Auditorium (Buffalo)	5	1	1	2	2
Indianapolis Coliseum (Indianapolis)	2	1	0	1	2
Pacific Coliseum (Vancouver)	5	0	2	2	2
Indianapolis Coliseum (Indianapolis)	2	1	0	1	2
The Omni (Atlanta)	2	1	1	2	0
McNichols Sports Arena (Colorado)	2	1	1	2	0
Capital Center (Washington)	2	1	1	2	2
Le Colisee (Quebec)	2	0	2	2	0
Joe Louis Arena (Detroit)	2	0	1	1	0
Northlands Coliseum (Edmonton)	2	0	0	0	0
Nassau County Veterans Coliseum (NY Islanders)	2	0	0	0	2
Winnipeg Arena (Winnipeg)	2	0	0	0	0
TOTALS	**1767**	**801**	**1049**	**1850**	**1685**

*New Madison Square Garden opened Feb. 18, 1968

Arena (Team)	GP	G	A	PTS	PIM
Olympia Stadium (Detroit)	78	40	51	91	107
Maple Leaf Gardens (Toronto)	28	8	18	26	25
Chicago Stadium (Chicago)	18	9	13	22	40
Montreal Forum (Montreal)	24	9	9	18	46
Boston Garden (Boston)	5	1	1	2	0
Madison Square Garden (New York)	3	1	0	1	0
Hartford Civic Center (Hartford)	1	0	0	0	2
TOTALS	**157**	**68**	**92**	**160**	**220**

"I was only 18-years-old and just drafted by the Red Wings, and casually, I remember Gordie just walking down the hall at Joe Louis Arena. Obviously, I recognized him, every Canadian would recognize Gordie Howe. He just was just down-to-earth and said, 'Hi, how are you doing?' For me, I was very nervous meeting him and somewhat intimidate because I knew who he was forever, so it was just a shock to see him in-person. He's very humble and a very easy person to be around. You're intimidated by the name initially, but as soon as you meet him he makes you feel comfortable.

"After my first year in Detroit I played in a charity hockey game out in Halifax, Nova Scotia. Of all things, I forgot my shin pads, and Gordie let me use his. I can't remember why he wasn't playing, but he said, 'Here, use mine.' I got to use his shin pads for a day and I think I returned them some time later that summer."

STEVE YZERMAN
Center, 1983-2006
Detroit Red Wings

From the
Rafters

SAWCHUK

1

1949-1955
1957-1964   1968-1969

LINDSAY

7

1944-1957
1964-1965

NUMBER RETIRED
March 12, 1972

HOWE

9

1946-1971

DELVECCHIO

10

1950-1974

ABEL

12

1938-1943
1945-1952

NINE